Sons of Isan

Taking Refuge in a Thai Temple

First published 2009
Second revised edition 2017
Edited by Dr. Reginald W. Holt
Cover art by Johnny Kutrip

ISBN 978-1-945905-04-9
Published by Tabla Press.
Subsidiary of Evenpath Press LLC.
www.evenpathpress.com

Sons of Isan

Taking Refuge in a Thai Temple

By
William Reyland

Author's Note

New to this edition are minor revisions to the text and the expansion of areas that may have been considered vague or unclear when first published. The author's insufferable naiveté and cultural ignorance of the time were left largely untouched.

There is a silent self within us whose presence is disturbing precisely because it is so silent: it can't be spoken. It has to remain silent. To articulate it, to verbalize it, is to tamper with it, and in some ways to destroy it.

Thomas Merton

1

Wai: Traditional Thai greeting

Wat: Temple

Kuti: Pali word for a monk's cell

A heavy tropical rain has begun to fall outside my cell and giggling flashes of orange robes hurry by my open door. A platoon of ants drink from my lukewarm cup of instant coffee, and mosquitoes attack my exposed feet where they feast on an area badly chafed by my sandals. I contemplate scratching, but it's already not healing very well. I decide instead to scratch around the area; the blood and filth blend into a flinty brown. I light a cigarette.

As evening begins to fall, the rain clouds burn off and reveal a giant Asian sun quivering midway on the horizon. Outside in the cambered light of the village, I hear the faint sound of water buffaloes shuffling along the outer wall of the temple, their hooves resounding like woodblocks on the steaming pavement.

Sprawled out, hot and in a stupor on the tile floor, I'm interrupted by a timid knocking at my door. There, in the darkness, stands Phra Suwatt, the abbot's secretary who has been in effect my welcome wagon monk since I arrived. He's twenty-three and has lived in this temple since he was a boy. He is tall and thin, so thin that his robes fail to define even the slightest physical feature. He's the only monk I've spoken to since my arrival the night before, while the other monks, as though fearful or painfully shy, keep their distance. Walking through the grounds, they gracefully flee to nearby buildings at my approach. Huddled in small groups, they peer and smile from the darkened doorways and teak framed windows.

Phra Suwatt enters my porch. As he does so, his face erupts into a warm smile. "Luang Por wants to welcome you, Ajarn Bill. He very happy you here at Wat Pramuenrat. Monk all happy today to see you. We want you stay long time. Please take a rest."

I thank him with a deep wai and before I can invite him in, he quickly departs. On my porch I notice he's left his sandals, but has already disappeared into the shadows; the looming, yet embracing shadows that only a Buddhist temple could cast.

Forty-eight hours ago I was in the States drinking coffee. I wish I had savored it more deeply because the majority of coffee here is instant. It seems trivial, doesn't it? It's not that I didn't do my research; on the contrary, I did plenty. This is the kind of place, however, that no amount of research can prepare you for.

Inside my cell, or kuti, I begin to unload my pack. In it are most of my possessions:

- Four pair of pants
- Six shirts
- Seven socks (not pairs, seven socks)
- Six pairs of underwear (I bought these soon after I arrived in Bangkok. They are very small despite the Medium tag. Never under any circumstances wear tight underwear in the tropics).
- Three ties
- A belt
- Toiletries (including anti-malaria pills I never got around to taking)
- A framed photographs of my son at the age of fifteen
- A camp stove (that I didn't need)
- A headlamp
- Assorted unframed pictures of my family
- Books: John Coltrane's biography, *Ascension*; a sailing dictionary; and Thomas Merton's *Seeds of Contemplation*)
- A few jazz CDs
- A Nikon and an additional lens
- Two pads of paper and two pens

Then there are things I haven't unpacked. Heavy, awkward, and odd-shaped, they are rational and irrational thoughts, beliefs and experiences. I tucked and crammed whatever I could of these into small, black nooks and crannies within myself.

Purging my life of my material possessions before I left home was more difficult than I was initially prepared for, but it was gradually freeing. The more that went out the door to charity trucks or to the curb, the easier it became. I recall the sound of my footsteps in the empty house, echoing off bare walls and hardwood floors. The last moment there was complete in spite of the emptiness. The bargain hunters gone, I strolled through empty rooms among bits of twisted newspaper and trails of dust hoping for a feeling, or a message, that I had made the right decision. I'd like to think that maybe a few particles of me still dance and drift in a beam of light on those hardwoods.

Locking the door for the last time, I wandered down the driveway and along the tree-lined streets. There was just the hint of fall in the air as I strolled through the fractured shadows of oaks. Fall in the Midwest is a beautiful thing to experience. I wondered when I'd see the next.

2

Phra: A title similar to Reverend
Ajarn: Thai word for teacher; title for addressing a teacher
Luang Por: When addressing an older esteemed monk as grandfather
Farang: Foreigner or westerner

As a convert to Buddhism, especially a western convert, I aim to approach it with a modern perspective. Because I wasn't raised Buddhist, or in a Buddhist country, my perception is tinged with romanticism. In the United States, my meditation was soft and quiet in clean halls and on cushions with other Westerners. None of it prepared me for this. First Lessons learned:

1. Thai Buddhism is many things, but it is not romantic or very soft.
2. Monks are people too.
3. Monks can't wear a watch, but they can carry a cell phone.

4. Some monks engage with society where they pursue degrees or work with communities, while many others remain very disconnected from society.

5. The view that many western Buddhists share, which sees Buddhism as a caretaker of nature, does not necessarily exist here.

When I was a child living in the Midwest, there was a carnival that came to my town every summer. It was your typical Midwestern fair with all the usual games of skill and cotter pin rides. They had a ride called the Rocco Plane. It was modeled after a Ferris wheel but scarier. I would go to the fair every day and watch as people got stuffed into the red, egg-shaped capsules before they were sent spinning and screaming skyward. I feared this ride so much that I waited until the last day of the fair to go on it. Being here in this far away temple feels just like sitting in that spinning Rocco Plane. I'm afraid but willing.

I'm having a hard time adjusting. The heat and the mosquitoes are unbearable. I still haven't been able to sleep for more than a few hours a night and often find myself chain smoking naked in front of the fan until sleep catches me.

I'm sure malaria originated in my bathroom. For a country with lingering malaria problems, they have an awful lot of standing water. I have a slimy trashcan full of it in my bathroom. I scoop it out with a yellow plastic bowl and after a brief eruption of irritated mosquitoes, pour it over my head or flush the squat toilet. I try not to imagine the epic orgies that take place upon the filmy surface.

Mornings in the temple are not always gentle and full of little tinkling Asian sounds. During my first morning, I thought the Burmese army was attacking before realizing an enormous bell was pounding away seemingly right outside my window. The intensity of this moment was soon punctuated by dens of howling temple dogs. It happens that the curious building I had seen the previous day was the temple bell tower with its bell house cleverly obscured by a low canopy of trees scarcely twenty meters from my cell.

If the bell fails to stir you, the nearly feral packs of dogs certainly will. There are dogs everywhere; inside the temple and in small packs that roam the streets. To my knowledge, there is no official animal control and euthanasia is not an option because Thailand is a Buddhist country. From what I understand, the local temples have become a sort of unofficial humane society.

There are twenty-five to thirty dogs at Wat Pramuenrat. Depending on a number of factors, such as the mating season and severe malnutrition, this number fluctuates. These are not necessarily domesticated animals. They reside in a sort of feral purgatory between domesticity and wild fury. There are daily battles over food and territory that can become absolutely violent, and it isn't unusual to see dogs with festering wounds. Most of the dogs aren't a real danger to humans, but there are a few I stay clear of. They are a real nuisance. They bark and quarrel at all hours of the night, dig up gardens in search of cool soil, and scare the Jesus out of the village children.

Of the many dogs that roam my area of the temple, one in particular took an immediate interest in me. She is a little yellow dog with a perpetually frightened expression. She loyally follows me wherever I go and sleeps directly in front of my cell at night. She also has a peculiar habit of bringing me a single leaf, which she randomly snatches from the ground and drops at my feet. Like the rest, she's acutely malnourished to such a degree that she's a walking anatomy lesson. I feed her and the other members of her pack whatever I can scrounge from the lunch trays. They seem to prefer fish. Since it has a lot of oils and proteins, I figure it's the best thing for them.

Wide awake from the bell episode and having recovered at least three of my five senses, I pulled on my jeans and ventured out to explore my new surroundings. All things considered, it was a beautiful morning. The sun was shining and it was only 100 degrees outside. Creaking open my door, I spied Phra Suwatt making his way to my cell. "Did you have a good sleep?" he asked.

"Well," I said, "it takes time to adjust to a new place. I did have a problem with the mosquitoes."

"Yes, (unapologetically) we found big nest in your room when cleaning. Please follow me to see Luang Por, and then eat food."

Taking me gently by the arm, which Thai males will often do, Phra Suwatt led me off to see Abbot Sunthorn, who is referred to as Luang Por, or venerable father. Betel nut is still popular among some elderly in Thailand, and Abbot Sunthorn, judging by his oxide grin, was obviously an avid chewer. Our abbot, who has been a monk for over forty years, is precisely what one would imagine an elderly abbot to be. His dark eyes peer out from a deeply lined and kind face, and while he easily erupts into laughter, he can be equally serious. He also has a particular fascination with President Abraham Lincoln and Dr. Martin Luther King, Jr.

As we entered his quarters, he was preparing a red clay plug that he unceremoniously stuffed into his mouth as I bowed three times in respect. Satisfied, he turned to Phra Suwatt and immediately began speaking rapidly through his blackened smile, intermittently laughing, spitting, and pointing in my direction while Phra Suwatt sat and listened stoically.

After a few moments, Phra Suwatt tried his best to translate. "Ajarn Bill, Luang Por says he wants you to stay forever and he can choose a good Thai wife for you." I wasn't exactly sure how to respond, so I simply asked Phra Suwatt to tell him how grateful I was for him letting me stay here. Luang Por responded by grunting something like, "Yeah, yeah," and then handed me a bunch of bananas. This was my cue that the meeting was over.

As we departed into the quickly invading heat of the morning, Phra Suwatt turned to me and said, "Luang Por says you look too tired so you should eat rice and take a rest. He also says he is happy you are here, but he worries about you wanting to leave.

Foreigners never stay and maybe eating and sleeping will be difficult."

Entering the main eating area, which is situated outside under a covered walkway near the bell tower, I finally got a good look at all the faces that had been trying so hard not to meet me. Seated at two long rows of tables were all of the twenty-seven ordained and eight novice monks of Wat Pramuenrat. Phra Suwatt made a casual introduction in Thai, and then in English, to the now cornered monks who looked on fearfully. What he said amounted to, "Okay, okay, this is Ajarn Bill. He came here to learn about the Buddha. Talk with him." Nodding, I then proceeded to make a general ass out of myself by attempting to wai each and every one of them when one greeting would have been sufficient. There were great smiles and a few random, "Hello, how are you?" greetings. Most of the monks, though, looked on bashfully and were reluctant to do little more than smile nervously or playfully jab one another in the ribs.

The laity is not permitted to eat with the monks and must wait until the monks have finished before they can partake in the leftovers (which are always plentiful). Finishing their meal, Phra Suwatt and the other monks left me in the care of three elderly Thai ladies. They hovered around me hemming and hawing as I sampled the various bowls of blazing Isan curries and cold fish. A few monks continued to stare at me from afar, trying to look busy whenever I happened to look up. A few who were unseen yelled, "How are you do!" followed by bursts of distant laughter. I think

20

I understand that Thai people are sometimes shy when it comes to foreigners, so I must remember to tread softly and smile often. I couldn't eat much of the food that morning, but my spirits were nourished.

Walking back to my cell to rest after breakfast, I saw three young novices milling about my doorway. Their robes, too big for their bodies, were bunched and knotted around their waists. They held curious-looking bamboo poles attached to what appeared to be tattered monks' robes. As I approached, one of them began frantically yelling what must have been a warning that the foreigner, or *falang*, was approaching. In a blur of orange robes, the three of them exploded off my porch in a flurry of screams and laughter. Fleeing en masse, one ran to an adjacent building. The other two simply dropped their mops and ran with arms and legs flailing, one losing a yellow plastic sandal in flight. Once inside, I noticed they had cleaned my floor.

My cell is the essence of simplicity. It is located in the back corner along a wall of the temple, and like the other buildings, is constructed entirely of concrete. It doesn't have running water, but it does have an attached bathroom, which must be entered from outside. Architecturally, my cell follows the ubiquitous temple theme with a sloping triangular roof.

Inside the plain interior, which measures roughly 15 x 20 feet, is a central mat where I have pillows for seating and a low table for writing. This mat also sometimes serves as my bed. There is also a massive antique bed made entirely of teak. As required by monastic code, it is no more than four inches above the ground and does not have a mattress. The only real amenity, other than a pot for boiling water, is an ancient red refrigerator that is a remnant from when Abbot Sunthorn occupied the cell some years ago.

Next to my cell is a small plot, or side yard. Fenced-in by the temple wall, it's one of the few private spaces in the temple. It is a kind of trash dump, but I'm transforming this area into a garden space. I spent a good week digging up garbage, shards of glass, moldy robes, and not surprisingly, a dog skeleton. I spend a lot of my time here in the mornings pondering design ideas and listening to the sounds coming over the wall of the awakening village.

With the novices sufficiently scared off, I kicked off my sandals and trod carefully over my still freshly mopped floor, which now gave off the distinct odor of wet dog. Sitting on my mat, I peeled an orange, and while lying on my back, I watched the ghostly cobwebs swaying gracefully from the ceiling. Overtaken by sheer exhaustion and lulled by the gentle hum of my fan, I slept.

3

This is not my first temple experience; it is, however, the first Thai temple that I've managed to survive in for more than two days. In 2003, my first trip to this region, known as Isan, ended abruptly as a result of a dietary disaster and what can only be described as a sort of catastrophic naiveté. On that occasion, I traveled to Thailand from the United States with a Thai monk I located in the phone directory.

I had been dabbling in Buddhist meditation and study for a few years. Although my approach was not very structured, my interest was profound nevertheless. What attracted me was the simple theory that through the practice of meditation and increased self-awareness, one is capable of transforming their relationship to the entire notion of life.

I had a fundamental understanding of Buddhism, but eventually I reached a point in my practice where my meditation was no longer something interesting, or even very enjoyable. I wanted to go deeper, but I was simply unable to do so. After many frustrated hours sitting half lotus, I decided I needed a teacher or spiritual guide.

Without starting a tirade about how provincial the Midwest can be, I'll just say the phone directory listings on Buddhism numbered two. One was called Wat Pharasarasatanaram. I decided any place with a name like that was worth checking out. One Saturday afternoon, feeling unproductive, I decided to investigate. It was here that I met Dr. Phra Maha Nikhom.

Phra Maha Nikhom, along with four other monks also from Thailand, resided in a Thai temple that was formerly a suburban Christian church located in an immigrant Thai community. The sign affixed to the double glass doors read, "Please remove shoe." This was the only indication that one was at a Thai temple. No attempts had been made to change the exterior of the building which sat neatly among identical ranch homes and resembled a Christian church in every way.

A second sign taped to the door directed me to "Ring Bell." Shortly, a trio of shaven heads appeared from within the darkened recesses, warily bobbing and peering from the shadows. One of them, an older monk, finally approached. Safely behind the thick glass, he looked me over awaiting an explanation. Smiling nervously and placing my mouth near the glass, I said, "A few days ago I called and asked if I might come here and talk to someone. My name is Bill."

"Oh," he said, raising his smoothly shaven brow. "Boy want speak with monk?"

"Yes. I called a few days ago and..."

"Boy wait," he said, disappearing into the darkened hallway.

Returning seconds later, he unlocked the door, and with a slight gesture, beckoned me to enter. Nodding to a row of simple, powder blue colored chairs, exactly the sort one would expect to see in a Christian church, he said, "Boy sit here."

Seating himself immediately across from me, he adjusted the upper folds of his saffron robes, and said to me, "Boy come to temple. Why?" Unsure of how to begin, I hesitated and then I explained that I was fascinated with meditation, and that I had been practicing for a while, but somehow wasn't getting very far. I told him something was missing and that I wanted to find it, whatever "it" was. All the while he sat listening with his hands clasped on his lap. When I had finished with my disjointed attempt to convey my desires, he simply grunted and said, "Sometimes boy come to temple very good; sometimes boy not good. He lost, drinking and smoking. Not have good life. He come see me, and I help him because I love him. I want him be happy. Sitting and walking with me, he change life and is happy. Are you drinking man?" he asked.

"No, I mean yes, I drink, but I'm here because I want to learn how to meditate. I want to learn more about Buddhism."

"You have wife?" he asked, wide-eyed.

"No, I don't. I haven't been married for many years. I have a son, though. He lives with me."

"Hmmm... very bad," he said. "Why wife not keep baby? How you take care?"

"Well," I replied, "it's complicated."

"You come here see me because you have trouble with your life. You not happy. You work hard for boy?" he asked.

"Yes," I said. "I work very hard, and we have a good life. I think he's happy."

"Hmm... You clean and make food for boy every day?"

"Yes, I do everything."

Adjusting his robes, he leaned toward me a little and asked, "Why you not get new wife?"

"Oh, maybe someday. Right now I'm in school and I have to work so I don't have the time."

Tilting his head back slightly, he thought for a moment and stated, "Sometimes boy come, have tired mind, too much stress, working hard make money, take care family. He come see monk and learn four noble truths, then he happy." He then rose from his seat and as he began to walk away, he said, "Follow monk."

We went inside what was once the main chapel and sat together in meditation. His words that day triggered something inside me. I was told to listen to my mind, to the constant noise, the confusion and grasping that, even while we sleep, churns away. Sitting across from me, I listened as he gently spoke of happiness and inner peace and relief from "self." Afterward, he gently cupped my forehead in his hands, peered into my eyes, and said, "You good man. You tired man. Be happy, you can. I love you."

The five years I spent among the monks and the Thai community eating with them, sitting in meditation, and even taking part in some temple activities, not only increased my curiosity about Buddhism but also the mysterious ways of Thai culture. Eventually, when the time was right, my curiosity would lead me far from my home and change my life forever.

When I broached the subject of traveling to Thailand, not as a tourist but to live in an actual temple, Phra Maha Nikhom's response was less than enthusiastic. "Hmm... boy go to Thailand temple? Temple not same. Food not same."

During the following year I convinced Phra Nikhom that I was ready and that it was something in my heart that I sincerely wished for, so in the middle of a Midwestern winter we packed our bags and boarded a plane bound for Bangkok. The first leg of a very long journey. With him in sandals and bundles of orange robes against the winter cold, and me buttoned warmly inside a pea coat and boots, we were an unusual sight. At the various airports, I made sure he had his meals at the proper times. Because he was too kind to ask for such things, I frequently offered him a variety of things to eat and drink. During our stopover in Los Angeles, however, he requested hot dogs.

While Phra Maha Nikhom slept comfortably curled up against the window, my head swam with expectations and increasing self-doubt. Behind me was everything I once knew and ahead of me, across the expansive Pacific Ocean, was the unknown. I worried about my son. Was he doing okay without me? Was I doing okay without him?

As we were going through customs, the officials greeted Phra Maha like a long-lost friend as he pressed items that I could not see into their hands. I learned later these were Buddhist amulets or charms featuring prominent monks and Buddha images worn for their perceived powers of protection.

Despite the fact that there were dozens of taxis queued up outside the airport, Phra Maha Nikhom had instead arranged for us a more rustic mode of transportation. He seemed giddy as he pointed out a blue pickup truck as it rolled up to the blackened curb. "Boy, my sister come take us. Take bag. Go in back. You okay? Hold on."

"Well," I thought to myself as the balmy air awakened my senses, "here I am in Thailand perched on a mountain of luggage at three in the morning in the back of a truck." Twenty minutes later, deep in the bowels of Bangkok, we pulled up to a small hotel.

Phra Maha Nikhom waited in the truck while his sister hurried me into the lobby, where a matronly and sleepy desk clerk copied my passport. Phra Maha's sister instructed me in no uncertain terms not to leave the hotel, "You stay here. You okay? You no go anywhere." She said good night and hurried to the waiting truck. I stood dumbfounded as they waved cheerfully and sped off. Blinking at my reflection in the hotel window, I waited for the sleepy bellboy as he searched a jangling pegboard for my room key.

My room possessed none of the quaint boutique decor of the lobby but instead looked like an outdated room at the Y.M.C.A. I had a tepid shower, and fell fast asleep on the hardest mattress ever produced for human kind.

We decided to stay in Bangkok for a few days so that Phra Maha Nikhom could rest and take care of the remainder of our travel plans. This gave me the opportunity to see some temples and meet up with Bill, an American friend who ran a successful law practice there and also possessed a wealth of cultural knowledge. I was eager for any advice Bill might have. More importantly, I wanted to know if he knew anything about where I was headed.

When I met Bill at the hotel, I told him that we were going to head up north to a region called Isan. His immediate reaction was, "Isan? You're going to Isan to live in a temple? Ah... Do you know what you're getting into?"

"Yeah, I think so. I mean, how could I know? I'll just have to try."

"Okay, I just want you to know, I've been up there many times, and it can be pretty rustic in the villages. I'll be impressed if you make it a week."

He was right, of course. I had no business going to Isan. Phra Maha Nikhom also had tried his best to warn me, but was unable to fully communicate what to expect. Even his sister, who took both of us out to see the sights, was concerned. During lunch at a noodle stall, she made it clear to me that she did not agree with her brother taking me to his temple and that it was a very bad idea. "Bill, my brother not know what he doing. Have bad food, no hospital for you."

4

At five A.M. and speeding northward, I was once again perched on the back of a truck watching the glittering lights of Bangkok fade behind a scrim of pollution. As we traveled beyond the city limits, I was immediately struck by the rapid transition from sprawling concrete chaos to the silent mosaic of rice paddies.

The fact that I really had no idea where we were going was no longer a concern. I had given up trying to get this information from Phra Maha Nikhom, who despite his best efforts had been unable to make sense of my map. By reading the highway signs and referring to my guidebook, I saw that we were at least heading in the right direction. A few hours after stopping to eat outside Khorat, we pulled into the city of Chaiyaphum where we picked up an ancient Thai woman. She sat next to me in the back and for the rest of the trip, happily fed me enormous sunflower seeds.

After our stop in Chaiyaphum, we left the highway and continued careening perilously down narrow secondary roads deeper into the backcountry. The secondary roads were mostly unpaved and completely washed out in many places. Making our way up gentle foothills, the rice crops gradually gave way to great stalks of sugar cane, which over the years had replaced what used to be an area primarily devoted to poppy.

Waving at the farmers, whose faces were heavily cloaked against the burning sun and choking dust, we made our way through the remote foothills leaving a contrail of fine, red dust in our wake. Finally, covered in red dust, we passed through a set of crumbling concrete gates into my home for the next three months.

Huddled up against seasonally barren rice paddies, the village, which was more like a hamlet, consisted of a dozen or so raised Thai houses in various states of decay. Under the houses, among huge ceramic water vessels so large a person could easily occupy one, chickens pecked and immense cattle stood vacant-eyed and oblivious. Along the main dirt road that was beaten down by the sun, old men wearing traditional checkered wraps of green, red, and white squatted under the trees.

My first impression of Wat Taksin was that it was nothing like the glittering, well-kept temples of Bangkok. The once stark white and vibrant reds here were now muddy and dull. The foundations were mud flecked. The temple wall had crumbled and was decayed in some areas. The gate, which at some point had been beautiful ironwork, had only one side intact. The other leaned precariously against a temple wall among a knot of weeds looping around it like little hands. Welcome to Isan.

At the temple, Phra Maha Nikhom was greeted with respectful wais by groups of chattering old ladies, while most of the men squatted around the fringes smoking cone-shaped cigarettes. He seemed very happy to be home once again in his village.

"Boy, you okay now? Happy?" he asked.

"It's nice to finally be here, yes." I replied.

"No problem. You wait here, monk go home, see mother. Okay?"

"Okay," I replied.

The villagers, apparently in shyness, also retreated, and left me to sit on the steps of the sala. It was quiet—a still, dusty silence. The other monks, if there were any, had yet to make themselves known. I began to wonder if the temple had been abandoned. It appeared to have been. Perhaps that's why the people were so glad to see Phra Maha Nikhom. They at least had one monk. At that moment, I saw three old monks at the far end of the grounds making their way through a tangle of dilapidated huts. They seemed to be heading right for me but made no indication of acknowledgement. I, too, made no indication, but as they grew nearer, I happily waied them and said, "Hello." One of them, with a very kind face of frosty stubble, immediately began to address me in halting English and leaning in for emphasis, he said to me, "I love you! I... love... you!"

This monk then abruptly displayed a sheet of paper that he produced from the recesses of his robes, on the front of which was a colorful advertisement featuring kittens and a ball of yarn. The old monk then pointed proudly at the kittens, smiled, and said, "I love kitten, hmmm... I love you!"

"Thank you!" I replied. "I love you."

"Sesechechee love you. Love kitten," he continued proudly. I assumed Sesechechee was his name because he repeated this several times while pointing at himself. Except for grunts and nods of approval, the other two monks said nothing but stood on beaming with delight.

Sesechechee then proceeded to rummage through his robes, this time producing a soiled legal size envelope containing several battered and filthy king sized cigarettes. Unfortunately, one of the conditions set forth regarding my stay was that I quit smoking, so with great pains, I reluctantly declined.

Satisfied with the exchange, the three old monks grunted something in Thai, to which I cheerfully responded, "Okay!" and they left me lingering in a marvelous cloud of stale smoke.

Alone again on the steps, I watched the chickens peck around the fringes of the village. Along the temple wall, there were several concrete game tables with crumbled checkerboard tops, and the broken benches set around them were propped up with chunks of other decaying tables. I watched as a small plastic bag skidded across the ground, snagging the underbrush and flapping in protest. I contemplated the dirt under my nails: the mingled filth of the journey from Bangkok. There was a yellowish stain on my ankle from riding seven hours in the back of a pickup. Highway dirt, and now the fine dust of Isan, coated my feet and stuck to my brow. I imagined the amount of mud my sweater could produce if wrung out. I stunk, and I really wanted Sesechechee, or whatever his name was, to come back so I could smoke.

After Phra Maha Nikhom returned, he led me inside the sala, one of only two buildings on the grounds. It was a vast, empty, and immaculate room devoid of furnishings. On the second floor of the sala lived a much younger monk with whom I would share a cell and who would also be my caretaker. He was very kind but seldom spoke.

Separated in half by a sagging bookcase, his cell consisted of a monk's bowl and random clumps of orange robes scattered about the floor like modern art. On the other side of the bookcase where I was to sleep, I was amazed to see a king size waterbed complete with padded rails and headboard shelving. The only thing missing was the water. Climbing into this at night was like sleeping in a coffin, although a coffin would have probably been more comfortable.

Dispensing with formalities and without a single word, my room-monk took up a tattered broom and began sweeping away wispy clumps of cobwebs that clung to the walls and barred windows. While he worked, I watched as they floated around before gently landing on his clean, brown scalp. From somewhere in the village, a rooster crowed and an old woman laughed. Transfixed by the moment, all I could do was stand there.

After I was settled, my room-monk led me back outside and directed me to sit in the bed of a waiting pick-up. A moment later, the other monks arrived at the sound of the temple bell. Setting their shoes on the tailgate, they climbed in beside me.

Sesechechee, who was beaming and apparently amazed to see me again, happily seated himself next to me. Two other elderly monks took me in without comment and for the remainder of the ride, conversed in hushed voices with occasional glances in my direction.

Lunch was not eaten in the temple but deeper in the village under a traditional teak house, which rested above us on massive teak posts. Here, the whole village had gathered to offer the monks their single meal of the day. Sitting among them upon a large central mat, I tried my best to appear comfortable as they unabashedly stared. From the platform where they sat, the monks, with the exception of Sesechechee who silently mouthed, "I love you," behaved as though none of us existed.

The food there was interesting. Using their bare hands, they transferred their offerings of rice into a central basket. This was then doled out, chanted over, and eaten by the monks. In my estimation, you were eating out of the hand of every person in the village—a village lacking soap dispensers, paper towels, and toilet tissue.

Despite this, I had decided that if I was going to live in Isan, I had to overcome my Western standards and get with the program. Clearly, no one there was dying of botulism, and despite the fact that the people were very poor, they were immaculate in appearance.

"Food not like in temple here, oh no, boy will see. Not good food there." I remembered these words as I sat and watched Phra

Maha Nikhom literally eat a stick. I followed his lead and gave it a try. It must have been some sort of herb, but it tasted of tree branch. The old women, who were truly fawning over me, and I loved them for it, seemed desperate in their attempt to feed me, or rather, unintentionally poison me. Smiling, they nudged numerous bowls of food toward me and made the universal sign for eating. I remember one dish in particular. Unlike many of the others, it looked delicious and resembled salsa, and in a way, it was. You could even say it was a kind of rice paddy salsa.

For the preparation of this dish, it's my understanding that when the rice paddies flood to the hilt and all manner of amphibious and otherwise water-born organisms are in their prime, a collecting screen is run through the water. Whatever is caught within the fine mesh is then mashed, pounded, and squashed into a slurry and combined with peppers and other spices. I call it "swim paste."

After the meal, which had yet to fully metastasize in my lower intestine, Phra Maha Nikhom asked me to address the village and announce my intentions. I'm not particularly fond of public speaking, but they all seemed so happy I was there and because they were so kind, I couldn't refuse. The whole village turned up in front of the temple for this. When I approached, I was shocked to see them lower themselves, and many, especially the elderly, had their hands clasped in a wai. Bewildered by this display, I looked to Phra Maha Nikhom who explained, "Thai people love and show respect in my village for foreigners."

In Thai culture, the practice of stooping is a show of respect and is based upon one's status. Keeping one's head lower is a way of communicating to others that you are not above them. This explains why many people dropped to their knees whenever Phra Maha Nikhom approached.

For my village address, I wanted the villagers to know first and foremost how grateful I was for their kindness. Phra Maha Nikhom translated this and then began taking questions. Most of these were from old ladies interested in my marital status. After answering a few questions regarding this, as well as ones relating to Thai food, I thanked them again, and after receiving an enthusiastic applause, went directly to the nearest squat toilet to puke.

After a night of dry heaving and lower bowel distress, I was up at dawn. As I lay watching a gecko traverse the grimy walls, I knew I was going to leave. Sick or not, I had no business being there. To think I had planned a whole year for this made me want to puke even more. I thought maybe I could puke some sense into myself.

Phra Maha Nikhom took one look at me as I sat upon the sala steps that morning and said, "Boy not happy today. Boy sick."

"Yes, I am not well."

"Hmm... no problem. I want you be happy. Boy go Bangkok see doctor."

"Phra Maha, I'm sorry. I know how much work it was to bring me here."

"Boy, quiet." With this, he spoke very gently and shaking his head, said, "Bill, monk only want you have happiness, not care about temple driving." Laughing, he continued, "You not understand. You come my home and everyone so happy; everyone love you."

At that moment, all I could do was look at his face with amazement. He had, in a mere few moments of supreme love, replaced my feelings of guilt and shame with calmness and acceptance.

"Boy, happy now? Get bag. Go Bangkok, see doctor." In my cell, I found my roommate monk opening a water-stained cardboard box and removing a medicinally suspicious looking bottle. After uncorking it, he poured out a glass and patted his stomach gesturing for me to drink. I threw back two healthy shots of whatever it was and was immediately and quite happily stoned. We stood looking at one another for a few moments and with a slight nod, he directed me to the door.

Downstairs with my bags, Phra Maha took me by the arm into the sala. In the sala, we prayed together in front of the main Buddha image. On my knees at his side, I silently made peace with myself. I thought of my parents and my family. Finally, before I placed my incense, I made a promise to myself, a promise that this journey was not over, but was just beginning.

Safely out of Isan, I returned to the chaotic clutch of Bangkok. After spending a week polluting my friend Bill's apartment and regaining my strength, I boarded a plane for a long and depressing flight home. Not actually having a home upon my less than triumphant return, I ended up sleeping on the various floors of friends and in my sister's travel trailer, which turned out to be smaller than a typical monk's cell.

What is it about living in a travel trailer that causes one to seriously reassess one's life? A few months later I found myself crossing the Pacific on the way back to Isan. I had to see this through, and if anything, my initial failure served to strengthen my resolve. I found my hunger for answers was even greater than before. I knew that the real challenge wasn't the food or living conditions, but something much deeper. None of which has much to do with spirituality. They were merely hurdles and well-placed obstacles.

Phra Maha Nikhom didn't blink when I told him I was going back. Maybe he knew I would. I wondered if my failure was part of some elaborate Buddhist lesson. "Boy, you want go back to Thailand? You go back. You find new Isan temple. You see."

Back in Isan, I stepped off my third class car in Nakhon Ratchasima, or Khorat, the gateway to Isan. My first time here I travelled under the guidance of a monk. This time I am alone and guided only by chance. It was by chance that I met a man named Boy who ended up becoming my personal driver for my first few weeks in the city of Khorat. I wasn't fifteen seconds on the platform before Mr. Boy had me gently by the arm. He had apparently decided to forgo the usual tuk tuk sales pitch in favor of simply apprehending his passengers directly from the platform. He easily charmed me out of the station and deposited me with ease into his tuk tuk. On our way into town, to let's face it, was essentially his hotel of choice, and what I'd hoped at least might include air conditioning, he related to me in a very mundane manner, as though it were a story he was telling outside of himself, the unfortunate night his wife hacked off his genitals with a meat cleaver, ran from the house, and threw them into a rice paddy.

5

Sala: Main hall for chanting, prayer and meditation
Bot: A sacred building reserved for religious rites and ordination
ceremonies

Thai Buddhism is basically composed of two distinct groups: forest monks (arannavasi) and city-dwelling monks (gamavasi). Forest monks concentrate primarily on meditation, while the city monks are primarily devoted to ecclesiastical studies. Wat Taksin, where I had my first experience, is a forest temple. It's also in a much poorer and desolate part of the country with few resources or educational opportunities. Those forest monks ate once per day, spent the majority of their time meditating, and lived a life of absolute poverty and reflection. At Wat Pramuenrat, formal and traditional education is central to the temple's mission. On any given week, the temple was abuzz with children and adults attending a variety of day or week-long meditation courses. In addition, the resident monks, with the exception of the elderly, are required to attend university full time. Because of these reasons, Wat Pramuenrat was a good fit. I knew it wouldn't always be easy, and I wanted a challenge, just as long it didn't involve swim paste.

I didn't have to go back to Isan. In fact, there were several temples located around the country, including those in Bangkok, that had programs designed specifically for foreigners. While these programs are probably more beneficial in a number of ways, they might fall a little short in terms of cultural immersion. Bangkok may be booming with culture and western influence, but in my estimation, the people of Isan possess a certain cultural purity, or "Thainess," and a level of warmth and acceptance that I've seldom encountered elsewhere.

One of the things that impressed me the most about this country is how omnipresent Buddhism is within society. Buddhism *is* Thailand; inextricably linked to society, politics, and the daily lives of ninety-eight percent of the country's inhabitants. Taxi dashboards are crammed with images of Buddha or revered monks. Homes, cars, businesses, births, marriages, and funerals are all brought forth with the assumed protection of a monk's blessing.

Some monks who are known for doing good deeds and performing magic are elevated to almost cult status. Protective amulets are cast in their image, and followers flock to their temples seeking their wisdom. Phra Maha Koon, an Isan monk, is beloved for his works of charity and unceasing ability to raise huge amounts of cash. If you go to his temple in Chaiyaphum, he will gladly step on your money, and if you're lucky, it will multiply.

There is a monk at Wat Pramuenrat who is referred to simply by his title, *Phra Maha*. He is loved and revered by the neighboring village whose inhabitants frequently come to the temple seeking his counsel. To my knowledge, he does not perform charity, and I've never seen him step on anyone's money. He doesn't seem to do much of anything.

Phra Maha, or "Great Monk," is a title bestowed on any monk who achieves a certain level of Pali language ability. The ancient language of Pali was the language believed to be spoken by the Buddha. A monk who achieves a level three Pali ability is given the title *Maha* or great. Phra Maha at Wat Pramuenrat is a level nine monk. A monk who reaches level nine is not rare, but because he achieved it at the age of twenty-two, it was highly unusual. He frequently and immodestly went to great lengths to remind me of his achievement.

I met Phra Maha briefly the night of my arrival. I found him sitting at a concrete table in front of his cell where he was typing on a laptop computer. It's difficult to describe monks because they all have similar features: no eyebrows, shaven heads and orange robes. Phra Maha, however, possessed a certain charisma and self-assuredness that seemed to set him apart.

"Hello, you must be Ajarn Bill," he said as I approached the table.

"Hello. You must be Phra Maha. It's nice to finally meet you," I said, greeting him with my hands raised in a respectable wai.

"Yes!" he said proudly and emphatically. "I am the great monk! I have been so busy that I've had no time to see you all day. Are you okay? Can you eat Thai food alright?"

"Yes, I am fine," I responded, taking a seat across from him.

"Good, good. I worry it may be too hot for you. Thai food is so hot," he said, laughing softly. "So, tell me. What do you think of Thailand?"

"Hot," I replied.

"I think so!" Phra Maha said. "The food is hot, the weather is hot, and everything is hot. So, you are from America. Is that right?" he asked, closing his computer with a soft click.

"Yes. I come from the Midwest state of Missouri. That is where I was raised."

Nodding in satisfaction, he replied, "I never been to America, but I have a plan to go maybe next year after my master's degree is finished. Ajarn Bill, Phra Suwatt told me you are interested in the Buddha. You know, we have many programs here for learning."

"Yes, I'm very interested in learning about Buddhism. It's the main reason I came. I think it's a beautiful way to live, and since Thailand is a Buddhist country, I thought this would be a good place to do it."

"Yes, Ajarn," he said. "That's why Thai people are so kind, especially to foreigner. They love to see foreigner. Phra Suwatt also say you want to help monks. Is that right?"

"Yes," I replied. "I would. I'd like to try and learn as much as I can and maybe help some people while I'm here."

"Actually," he said, leaning back and adjusting his robes, "I have a special project for you that I was hoping you can help me with. I am working hard on a special master's degree and I need you to help me with the English. What do you think?"

"Oh, of course, Phra Maha," I responded. "I would be more than happy to take a look at it."

"Excellent, Ajarn, I am so happy you are here. We don't see many foreigner, and we never have a teacher, so we are very lucky. I think we will be very good friends!"

"I think so too. Thank you."

"For your happiness, Ajarn. You should go now and take a rest and we talk more tomorrow."

The next morning, still exhausted from the previous week of travel and still not sleeping well, I lay on my mat, listening to the clamor of the awakening village. Roosters crowed as the acrid smell of cooking fires drifted in through my open windows. On the other side of the wall, motorcycles screamed by and shot out of the village beginning a miserably hot day on the Khorat plateau.

With little hope of sleeping, I made lukewarm instant coffee and went out to my porch in time to catch the morning broadcast. Many villages in rural areas have a public address system. Ours crackled to life every morning between six and seven o'clock when a tinny distorted monologue erupts. This lasted about ten minutes and was typically followed by Luk Tung, or traditional Isan folk songs. Luk Tung are a kind of Thai blues, which lament and celebrate the toils and beauty of country life. I later learned that the broadcast was a morning sermon or pep talk, and in many villages, it was broadcast from the local temple. As a musician, I found it an agreeable way to start the day.

As I listened, I saw Phra Suwatt making his way along the path, approaching my cell. He had a big smile on his face and before reaching me, he announced eagerly, "Ajarn Bill! All monks go to another temple to hear special monk. Monks want to know if you go too."

There was apparently a young monk who was going to recite from memory all of the 227 monastic precepts and many monks from the surrounding provinces were gathering there to share in the experience.

I was eager to join them.

"Yes, I would love to go. What time are we leaving?" I asked.

"Monks go at one hour. I will come for you."

Ten minutes later, I was barely dressed when I heard Phra Suwatt banging on my door, though normally he knocks very quietly. "Okay, okay," he said. "We go."

It is not uncommon in Thailand to see an entire family perched comfortably, albeit precariously, on one motorcycle. They maximize any mode of transportation to carry as many people or animals as possible. I've seen as many as five people on one motorcycle. Today, fourteen monks and one slightly emaciated white guy would travel together in the cramped bed of a pickup truck. Since nothing breaks the ice like forcing fourteen people into the back of a truck, I imagined it would be a good opportunity to get to know them. It turned out to be a pivotal moment.

Crammed together in such close quarters and with no chance of escape, many of them began whispering and encouraging each other to speak to me. Before long, a Khmer monk pointed at my legs and asked, "Oh, Teacher Bill, how you sit like that?" With this bold question, the façade of silence had suddenly broken down and then came the questions.

"You have wife here?"

"Where is your home?"

"You very handsome man."

This continued as we bounced along the narrow country roads and through the parched rice paddies while passing inquisitive buffalo and smiling villagers (or was it smiling buffalo and inquisitive villagers?). It was a breakthrough and did much to strip away my loneliness.

Thailand has Buddhist temples like the West has McDonald's. There are thousands of temples in Thailand. We must have passed at least two dozen temples and to my great disappointment even a McDonald's. By the time we had arrived at the temple we had become an animated mass of laughter rocketing down a country road. We arrived at the temple in a cloud of laughing dust. The parking area was spilling over with a thousand shades of yellow as we pushed our way through the sea of smiling faces and made our way up a massive set of stairs leading to a magnificent sala.

Four main temples were taking part in this event, each having their respective abbots in attendance. When visiting a temple for any reason, one must adhere to a strict manner of dress and behavior. As a foreigner, it was important that I learn and follow these important rules. Phra Suwatt made sure to brief me accordingly.

Of the many rules related to socializing with monks, a significant and critical one is that one's head must not be higher than theirs. The monks normally sit upon a raised platform within the temples. When the people, however, sit on mats among the monks, they hunch their shoulders or bend slightly forward in an effort to make themselves lower than the monks. This posturing is a direct correlation to where you fit in the social strata, and I frequently saw this posturing acted out in public. It is considered polite to stoop a bit when walking past or standing next to elderly people, who are treated with a higher level of respect.

When addressing a monk, it's also necessary to use a specific language. In the case of an older monk, one uses the word *Luang Por*, or venerable father, and for a younger monk, *Than,* or venerable. When formally visiting an abbot, one should perform three bows while on your knees with your palms down and your head not quite touching the floor. Traditional scriptures mandate that the right hand touch the floor slightly before the left. Each bow should conclude with a wai raised just below one's nose. I do this every time I go to sit with Abbott Sunthorn, and though it may seem a bit much, it's merely a sign of my respect.

After my lesson in Thai social etiquette, Phra Suwatt escorted me into the eerily quiet and cavernous sala. A few monks were preparing an area around an elaborately carved and uncomfortable-looking armchair. Sitting mats were scattered around the ornate chair. On top of a battered, low reading table was a weathered and heavily bookmarked volume of Buddhist scripture.

In the midst of this activity stood a remarkably thin monk, murmuring to himself in preparation for the spectacle to come. With great distinction, this monk was able to recite all 227 vinyana precepts from memory, which are the rules and regulations that a monk must use to govern himself.

Along the back wall sat four abbots like four orange peas in a pod. Sufficiently coached, I sat down on the floor in front of them. Nervously, and with as much grace as I could muster, I performed three respectful bows while on my knees. The abbots were wide-eyed with astonishment and began to excitedly converse with Phra Suwatt.

Always my faithful translator, Phra Suwatt said, "Ajarn Bill, monks say you have good manners for a farang. They want to know how you feel today and if you can eat Thai food?"

I replied, "Luang Por, I think this place is very beautiful and Thai food is delicious."

"Okay, okay," replied Phra Suwatt. "They want to know if Ajarn Bill want wife? Thai wife always take care of man, and they think you should be married. Also, they say you very handsome."

"Thank you," I replied. "I don't know about a wife—maybe after I leave the temple." Phra Suwatt continued, "Excuse me, they want to know when you will become a monk?"

"Well," I said, "I'm not sure, but it's only a possibility. I have a lot to learn."

"Hmmm... I think so," replied Phra Suwatt. "Okay, okay, we watch special monk now. Come, come," he said, leading me away by the arm.

Many situations involving the presence of monks traditionally begin and end with chanting. Typically the monks chanted every morning to begin the day, before and after every meal, and again in the evening. In the evenings, the monks usually gathered themselves into the tiny bot or prayer room across from my cell. I would often wander around outside and listen. The candlelight flooded from the open shutters like a golden vapor.

As the chanting started marking the beginning of this event, I sat gazing at the huge gilded Buddha surrounded by twinkling yellow candles while gentle swirls of incense mingled with my senses. As they chanted with their hands in prayer around me, I contemplated these men who detached from the world and chose a path between the right and the left: *the middle way.* I wanted what they had. I wanted to learn how they do it, how they laugh so easily, how they walk and move with such calm. I wanted my eyes to be clear and smiling again. I thought about these things in this place so far from home, so far from anything I've ever imagined yet so close to my heart.

After the chanting ended, everyone, except me, moved to the perimeter around the chair. The monk, who would recite the precepts, seated himself. After a wai to his fellow monks and with his hands in the prayer position, he cleared his throat and began. Unlike the chanting, this resembled singing. As he raced along without pausing, an elderly monk kept pace by book marking each recited passage.

After nearly an hour, I was overwhelmed and in considerable pain from reverently sitting in the half lotus position. Phra Suwatt, my watchful minder, crept over and whispered into my ear, "You should go out and take a rest." I was hesitant to call attention to my weakness, but because he insisted, I hobbled on numb legs out into the sun.

Outside the sala, I found a group of very young novices who were setting up long rows of tables with soy milk, fruit juice, and hundreds of bottles of Coca-Cola. The moment they saw me descending the stairs, they went into a panic and fled. Helping myself to a bottle of soy milk, I sat down to take some notes in my journal and wait them out as they looked on from under the shade of a nearby tree. Eventually, one of them stealthily came over and stood behind me. Looking over my shoulder, he peered at the pages of my journal while keeping his hands behind his back and leaning in from as far away as possible in case he needed to flee. Not wanting to spook him, I flashed a smile and continued to write. After a few moments, he said, "Hello, I am fine."

Turning to meet his gaze, I responded in kind to which he enthusiastically answered, "Thank you very much!"

The rest of the novices, confident that I meant them no harm, cautiously came over to investigate. Over bottles of soy milk and Coca-Cola, they inspected my bag and my journal, picking out words and laughing hysterically. An older boy, who looked about twelve years of age, repeatedly asked me for a cigarette but was denied. It was a reminder that I too must quit this disgusting habit.

6

Sangha: The community of monks and laity

I was extremely happy that I had decided to return to Isan and felt as though I was slipping into all of this rather gracefully. The tropical heat was losing its edge, and I could almost feel my body beginning to adapt. Even my angry bowels were beginning to settle.

Living in the temple was still very much like living on another planet. The climate, food, and all things sensory are completely different. Physically and mentally tapped, I slept through the rest of the day, and in the morning, even the bell failed to stir me.

Buddhist temples are public places in Thailand. When one of the many Buddhist holidays or festivals takes place, the temple is often overrun with people. There were many mornings when I had to press my way through crowds of Thai families who unabashedly stared at me. This was not a pleasant way to start the day.

I'm a morning person. I love getting up to a sunny day; I just need a few minutes of solitude. In order to ensure my morning solitude, I developed a routine. The first thing I did before venturing outdoors was look to see if any visitors were in the immediate area. Except for monks, this would be unusual. Most of the visitors congregate in the front of the temple away from the monks' cells. One morning, however, I walked straight into a gaggle of old ladies while wearing only a small towel. If they were there to earn merit, I'd say they got a bargain.

After making an initial check, I proceeded to my porch which afforded me a greater view of the front area of the temple. If there were any events, I would know about it. If the temple was clear, I was free to do my rounds which involved doing my walking meditation at the crematorium and meeting with Luang Por for coffee.

My second option was to avoid the front of the temple altogether and go the back way around the temple lake. The only obstacle to this route was an unruly pack of dogs. If I was quick enough, I could cross the main road past prying eyes and go to the crematorium. This route carried the added advantage that few Thai would hang out at a crematorium. There are too many spirits lurking about.

This might seem like a lot of work, if not slightly neurotic, but I was an oddity to those curious Thai people. I love them; I really do. They are the warmest people I've ever encountered on my travels, but a whole crowd of them staring at me in the mornings or wanting to talk to me about Thai food was just too much. I felt like a celebrity and I hated it.

On rare mornings when few people were in the temple, I usually wandered over to Luang Por's cell and drank his fresh-ground coffee, a real treat because Thais tend to prefer instant. Holding our steaming glasses of coffee, we usually just sat there grunting and smiling at each other. Although one morning, he put his hand over mine and told me he loved me.

Luang Por is not only a model of monastic purity, but a fascinating and lovely man as well. As the ecclesiastical head of his sub district within the province of Nakhon Ratchasima, he is responsible for overseeing a host of education programs and various traditional monastic responsibilities. It's his commitment to education, and in broader sense, the future, that sets Wat Pramuenrat apart from some other temples where, aside from dogmatic responsibilities and rituals, the monks seem to do little to advance Thai society.

This forward view or philosophy makes Abbot Sunthorn uncommonly progressive by all accounts. He is on a personal mission to bring Thai Buddhism, which in recent years has been faltering and in a steady decline in the face of progress, into a modern and increasingly globalized Thai society.

While economic development and the weight of the burgeoning middle class are factors in the decline, what is most damaging to this traditional and deeply cultural way of life is the sangha itself. In recent years, the sangha, or community of monks, has been rocked by incessant and widely reported cases of corruption, embezzlement, and other less pious activities.

One case involved an abbot who allegedly gambled thousands of dollars on World Cup matches. There was another case in which a monk dressed in woman's clothing was apprehended by police at a karaoke parlor. As a Westerner, I concede that my perspective is tinged with romanticism founded in a natural American perception that Buddhist culture must be innately ascetic. I found the stories shocking. After all, it was the image I had of the monastic life that brought me here.

Abbot Sunthorn believes, and I agree, that in order for Buddhism to sustain itself through these changes, monks must be properly educated. If the people who enable the temples to stay in operation through their contributions no longer feel connected to the sangha, the temples will fall into ruin.

Gone are the days when the temples were the central hub of village life. Before the modernization of public school systems in Thailand, education was primarily administered within the local temple. This maintained a close bond between the village and monastic community.

Wat Pramuenrat offers a variety of specifically designed meditation courses. Children also frequently attend meditation camps and other workshops that emphasize moderate and compassionate lifestyles, which are the cornerstones of Buddhism.

At Wat Pramuenrat, I had a real opportunity to embrace not only an entirely new way of living but, more importantly, I had a vehicle to bring me out of myself and actively engage the people, not as a bystander peering through a camera lens, but as an active participant.

With the help of Phra Suwatt and Phra Maha, we would soon begin an English teaching program inside the temple. The main focus of the program would be to educate the resident monks.

The second part of the program would focus on the children in the local village who, because of economic reasons, are often unable to study at expensive language schools. Most of the children in Thailand study English, but the primary focus is on grammar due to lack of native English speakers. For this reason, Thai students have very little opportunity to take part in English conversations. Keeping in mind I was not a trained professional, my goal was not necessarily to just teach them the language, but also build their confidence by giving them an opportunity to speak and spend time with a native speaker.

Before we could begin teaching the village children, I required the blessing and permission of the "Poo Yai Ban," or the village "head man." Even as a guest in the temple, I was obligated to make his acquaintance. The "Poo Yai," as he is more commonly referred to, is responsible for local projects, organizing Buddhist holiday activities, and keeping order in the village. It's "his" village and nothing happens without his knowledge, and consent. This includes the White guy in the temple.

My first impression of our head man was that of a very self-confident and severe man. At his request, I met him one morning in Luang Por's cell. After we waited nearly an hour, Poo Yai, with barely a glance, even at Phra Suwatt, strode in with an air of defiance and took a seat on the floor across from me. Phra Suwatt made my introduction and with the understanding that he was a man to be respected, I gave him a suitable wai.

While most Thais do their best to welcome strangers, the Poo Yai looked at me with a mixture of disdain and suspicion. After a brief conversation with Phra Suwatt, Poo Yai departed. He didn't seem all that happy to meet me.

"Ajarn Bill," said Phra Suwatt, "Poo Yai thinks you are CIA."

"What?" I asked, laughing. "He thinks I'm CIA?"

"Yes. To him, it's difficult to know why you want to stay here. He does not understand."

7

Rising, the sons and daughters of Isan wash the dust from their smiling eyes. In the fields they tread their hopes into the reluctant soil, dreaming of sustenance. This region typically has only one growing season due to the climate, and the majority of the farming is still largely un-mechanized. From my garden bench, I could see the farmers crouched and bent at the waist in the distant rice paddies as they tended to their individual plantings. Across plains of green, the sun rose and fell within this backdrop of human toil.

From the opposite side of the wall, I heard the wooden cowbells of water buffalo on their way to accept their daily burden of the yolk and the thwack of their keeper's whip against their muscled flanks. The keeper sang out, "Aaap, aaap!" As they passed, I peeked over the wall and was a little surprised to see him riding a bike.

Isan is situated between Laos and Cambodia, and, in the course of history, has been ruled by both nations. This region has historically been a land of people marginalized by war and poverty.

The first major civilization in this region of Thailand was that of the Mon people. Settling in the 6th century, the Mon were part of the Indian culture known as Dvaravati who many believe were responsible for introducing Buddhism to the region. Their influence can be seen today throughout Thailand in the architecture and artistic motifs. In the eleventh century, the Mon was displaced by the more powerful Khmer empire from the city of Angkor. The Khmer built a number of temples along the ancient Khmer Highway, most notably in the Thai cities of Phimai and Phanom Rung.

The rule of the Khmer lasted until approximately 1238 A.D. when the Sukothai Empire, breaking away from the Khmer Empire, began forcing them back to Cambodia, fragmenting Isan into individual statelets or "mueang."

The Lao dominance was further intensified with the fall of the original Siamese capital of Ayutthaya to the Burmese, resulting in the establishment of a new capital farther south in Bangkok.

The influence and predominance of Lao culture in the twentieth century prompted the Thai government to assert its control over Isan through a program termed "Thaification." This program attempted to replace the Isan language with Thai through radio and television broadcasts, as well as create a newly designed school system that would supplant the instruction typically provided by the monks.

Due to the rising fear of Communism in the 1960s and the region's abject poverty, remoteness, and history of independence, the Thai government perceived Isan to be a likely breeding ground for Communist activity. Fearing this threat, and armed with evidence of activists and equipment entering the country from Laos, the Thai government allowed a number of American military bases to be established around the region. It was also widely believed that covert CIA operations against the Communist insurgency were very active in the region. Perhaps this is why Poo Yai suspected me of being an undercover operative of the CIA.

One of the largest of these military bases was based in Khorat. The GIs, some of whom never left, can still be seen today hunched over the bar at the still-active V.F.W. Although American troops pulled out many years ago, the installation is in operation, and from what I understand, still hosts joint training exercises with American and Thai troops. The existence of these bases had much to do with improving highway transportation and for the first time, linked Isan to the rest of the country.

8

Of the many new things I struggled with while living in Thailand, one of the most difficult for me to fully comprehend was the apparent lack of concern for the environment. Very often the air around the village would be filled with a kind of black dust that I imagine was fallout from the numerous plastic-fueled garbage fires that smoldered in and around the temple. I saw a lot of plastic floating in the waterways and drifting along the roadways. When traveling to other more prosperous regions, I noticed a slightly higher level of cleanliness.

I appointed myself as the environmental caretaker of my area. This involved disposing of the many plastic bags snagged among the gardens and the half-filled, decomposing ones that the dogs dragged around and constantly fought over.

I replaced the slimy bathing trashcan in my bathroom with a covered model and tied the old one to a post. It didn't make much of a difference because a lot of the garbage was simply discarded onto a central pile near the lake. When set ablaze, it emitted an inky toxic odor that smoldered for days.

When I lived in the United States, Sunday was always cleaning day and the same was true in the temple. I spent my

Sundays doing laundry in a huge chipped enameled bowl, weeding the garden, and cleaning out the copious amount of dust that accumulated in my cell. After I mopped my floors and watered the gardens, I retired to lounge on my little tiled porch to meditate or look at the Thai newspapers that I couldn't understand.

My porch is completely surrounded on three sides by wrought iron bars, deftly bent into a cat's cradle of meandering lotus blossoms. Often, in the middle of the night and affected by heat-related insomnia, I stood there safely enclosed while staring through the bars like a criminal scanning the dark.

One evening I went out to my porch to cool myself upon the tile. Everyone told me that it wasn't safe to wander around the temple at night, but despite this advice and for the fact that there was a beautiful full moon, I exited the porch to sit on my bench beside the garden.

Three feet from the bench, the roar of a speeding motorcycle outside the temple wall startled me. Through the decorative open spaces, I watched as it skidded to stop, whipped around, and sped away. I was more puzzled by this than shaken.

In the shadows, I saw a dark figure clumsily clamber over the wall and land among the tangled underbrush. Standing in the moonlight, I contemplated making a dash for my cell. Instead, I remained still. Heaving with labored breath, the figure momentarily stood motionless before crashing through the trash-strewn regions behind Phra Maha's cell.

As I retreated to the safety of my porch, I was again startled by the sound of the motorcycle, but this time it was speeding into the temple. Leaping inside my porch, I glimpsed the rider, whose face was concealed by a red bandana and mirrored sunglasses. As the motorcycle idled down the concrete path, I hid in the shadows as the headlights raked across my walls. Throttling up, it sped off through the darkened temple. I locked my door once inside my cell, and after a few moments of calm, it began to occur to me that the person who jumped the temple wall might have been in danger. Still rattled, but no less curious, I decided to fetch my headlamp and look around. At this point, the dogs were wide-awake and happily followed me as I fearfully crept into the alley behind Phra Maha's cell. Looking on dumbly, the dogs stood around my legs as I shone the light among the knots of weeds and garbage. If anyone had been there, the dogs would have attacked them in seconds. Satisfied with my search, I gave the dogs a good scratch and then promptly went back to my cell.

I thought someone should know about the intruder, so the next morning I went to see Phra Maha. I knocked on his door, and he emerged disheveled and sleepy.

"Oh, Ajarn Bill why do you wake me?"

"Good morning, Phra Maha. I thought you would be up. I'm sorry."

"Ajarn Bill, I was up so late working on my thesis, so now I sleep late. Is everything okay?"

"Yeah, I guess. I did want to let someone know that last night I saw a person jump over the wall and run through the temple."

"Hmmm," said Phra Maha, stretching his plump body. "Well, I'm sure everyone is okay. Ajarn, you should not be out at night. It can be very dangerous."

"In a temple?" I asked.

"Anywhere can be dangerous. We never know."

"Okay. Well, I just thought it was strange, and I thought someone should know."

"Of course, Ajarn Bill, for your happiness."

Leaving Phra Maha's cell, feeling somewhat perplexed by his lack of concern, I headed off for my morning meditation behind the crematorium. I briefly paused near the bell tower to greet a group of Khmer monks who had only lately stopped fleeing in my presence.

Many of the monks congregate in this area because it is central to the dormitory and the outdoor eating area. This is also where I first met Phra Samboen, who quickly became a very dear friend and confidant.

In an act of courage that none of the other monks had ever displayed, he gleefully called out to me as I passed under the elevated porch of his cell.

"Hello! Teacher Bill! How are you today?"

It took me a moment to realize where this exuberant voice was coming from until he again called out, "I am here, Teacher Bill!"

Looking up, I saw an extraordinarily tiny and thin monk smiling down upon me from the porch of a traditional Thai house. One of only two of such houses remaining in the temple, these are raised high off the ground and constructed of hand hewn teak. I offered this friendly monk a suitable wai, he continued...

"Teacher Bill, is it okay if I ask where you come from?"

"I come from the United States."

"Oh, that is a good place I've never been. Someday I want to go see," he said excitedly.

I looked up and shielded the sun from my eyes as I tried to think of a careful response. "Well, America is great, but I think Thailand is a fine country."

"Oh, no, Teacher Bill," he said, shaking his head as he smiled. "I think America is much better than Thailand. Thailand is poor, and your country is so rich. You can have everything."

"Well, yes. America may have money, but it's not as easy as people think."

"Teacher Bill," he asked, leaning over the railing, "May I ask you to come in?"

"I would love to," I said. "Thank you."

Phra Samboen said, "Excuse me, again. My English is not so good. Would you please come in and sit down for a moment?"

"I understand," I said, laughing. "Yes."

Climbing the steps past a thin, dusty chicken perched upon the railing, I met him upon the porch and removed my sandals. The rough-hewn beams, polished by countless bare feet, had the feel of warm, firm leather.

The windows, without glass or screens, had the simplicity and function of a barn. Leading me off the porch, Phra Samboen eagerly invited me into his little room and said, "Teacher Bill, please come in. Sit down! Do you want some milk? Are you hungry?" Moving quickly, he reached into his alms bowl, pulled out an assortment of boxed UHT milk and several bakery items, and proudly placed them on the gleaming wood in front of me. "Here, I save these for you. Everyone worries about you being hungry so the monks say we should save things that have good taste for you."

"Thank you, but I'm really okay, and I think I shouldn't eat in front of you."

"No, no, it's okay," he replied. "You are my friend, and we don't act so serious when we are here, okay? I will make coffee to drink with you. I am so happy you come here to see me. Every day I want to come see you, but I am afraid to bother you."

Sitting across from me on smooth teak with his steaming juice glass of instant coffee, Phra Samboen adjusted his robes, leaned in, and asked me in a most direct and uncharacteristically Asian fashion, "Teacher Bill, I'm sorry. Why do you come here? All monks want to know."

Phra Samboen listened intently as I replied, "In the United States, I have a son who is now eighteen and living his own life. Being free to travel, I decided to come to Thailand. My teacher, an Isan monk, brought me here before and I fell in love with the people. I wanted to come back to see if I could help and also to learn more about the Buddha. When I heard that Luang Por wanted me to stay, I moved right in."

"Teacher Bill, you are Christ?" he asked, cocking his head slightly.

"I'm sorry," I replied. "Am I Christ?"

"Yes," he said, adjusting his robes. "Are you Christ man? Like people from your country?"

"Oh!" I exclaimed. "You mean Christian?"

Phra Samboen, who tends to giggle like a schoolgirl, held his hand over his mouth to contain himself. "Oh, Teacher Bill, I am sorry, please forgive me! Yes, I mean to say Christian. So... are you Buddha?"

"Yes," I replied, laughing. "A few years ago, I met a Thai monk in my hometown and learned about Buddhism from him, and now I am Buddhist."

"Teacher Bill," he said more seriously. "I did not know this, but I think you are a good man to come. Before, when I heard this, I was very excited and now I am happy to talk together with you."

"I'm very excited, too. It's been a crazy time so far and everyone here has been so kind to me."

"Hmmm... I think so," he said, smiling. "Teacher Bill, Phra Suwatt say you will teach English. I want to ask to be your student. Is that okay?" he asked hopefully.

I replied, "Yes, of course. Phra Maha and Phra Suwatt are trying to find a good time to start classes, so maybe in a few weeks. We're also planning a village class for the children and anyone else who wants to learn. It should be fun! Everyone is welcome."

"Okay, Teacher Bill, I have to go for chanting with monks. Thank you for speaking with me. I am so happy today talking with you."

"Me, too, Phra Samboen," I said while rising to leave.

As I descended the stairs, Phra Samboen looked down on me and beamed, "Please come see me whenever you want! Bye, Teacher Bill. Have a nice day."

Phra Samboen is one of a small group of monks originally from Cambodia. They stick very close to one another in the temple and seem to be an almost separate culture. The majority of these monks grew up during Pol Pot's bloody revolution and have similar stories of poverty, war, and death. Nearly all of the monks lost at least one family member during the violent revolution. Their studies and dedication to Buddhism would turn out to be a great source of personal inspiration during some difficult moments. Remembering their tales gives me pause when I feel like life hasn't been fair. As a Westerner, I'm increasingly aware I often feel entitled and easily frustrated when things don't go my way. It's one of the many lessons I would learn as a person with a Western mind staying in a Thai temple.

9

Many of the monks of Wat Pramuenrat have been in the temple since they were young boys. As a solution to the poverty and otherwise bleak future in their villages, the temples offer them opportunities for a college education, a better standard of living, and for some, upward mobility.

Thai families who give their children over to the temple do not do so with a heavy heart. They take tremendous pride in the fact that their sons are monks. This not only brings status to the family but, as the Thais believe, also earns them merit for the next life.

The type and extent of education one receives at a temple is determined by the abbot's particular philosophy. Some abbots, like Abbot Sunthorn, are very progressive and believe in a well-rounded and modern education. Others, however, focus more heavily on the Pali language and Buddhist scripture.

Wat Pramuenrat monks attend daily classes at Mahachulalongkorn Rijvidyalaya, also known as "MCU," which is a Buddhist university located on a plain of rice paddies outside the city of Khorat. This relatively new university was built with private funds raised primarily by the much beloved Isan monk, Phra Luang Por Koon, whose giant golden image can be seen adorning the apex of the administration building.

As Phra Maha's reluctant driver, I spent a good deal of time at this institution where I mostly waited in the heat for Phra Maha, whose liberal concept of time was a source of frustration for me. I had the opportunity to converse with the friendly university staff who found it odd to see a White man driving a temple van.

One of the staff members who frequently conversed with me was the head of the English department. As it turned out, he happened to be in need of an English teacher. Can you imagine the luck? Having the opportunity to teach in the Buddhist University was an amazing stroke of good fortune, not only as a new teacher in need of experience, but also as a means to immerse myself even deeper within the monastic culture.

I taught on Tuesday afternoons. I drove not only myself but also fourteen student monks who crowded, some happily and some fearfully, into the back of our aged temple van. In the beginning, this was a daily adventure fraught with their gasps of fear and surprisingly at times, a great deal of laughter. Except for a very reluctant third-gear and a misplaced steering wheel, the needed equipment was there and I eventually got the hang of it.

All kidding aside, driving anything in Thailand is incredibly dangerous. It seems that the moment Thais get behind the wheel, they become instantly unaware of their surroundings. Farmers with rusty tanks of butane lashed to their motorcycles career perilously about. Traffic signals are regarded with a passing interest. Entire families squeezed onto a single scooter creep along the thin shoulder against the flow of traffic.

Once we left the main road and entered the countryside, the Buddhist University of Mahachulalongkorn Rijvidyalaya rose from the surrounding rice paddies like a monolith. I always sighed in relief as we made this turn because it meant we had all survived another day. From a distance, clusters of orange robes milled about the terraces and open-air corridors. I don't think I have ever seen so many monks in one place at the same time. There was a special vibe there that radiated a current of kindness and good will that filled the whole place with a feeling of lightness and joy.

To be fair, the educational system in Thailand has come a long way, but there is still work to do that requires some finishing touches. I found it rather surprising that the monks are habitually late for class. Often inviting any kind of debate or discussion, no matter the subject, was met with an eerie silence. I attribute this to the fundamental Thai teaching methodology that seemingly discourages independent thinking, and instills the belief that direct questioning of a teacher is disrespectful. What I thought was interesting, the students found dull. They would sigh heavily in class and exclaim, "Ajarn Bill, too serious!"

I learned that young men without any previous sexual experience would rather talk about girls. I eventually gave up attempting to prepare a lengthy lecture and turned what was supposed to be a media class into an English conversation class.

Despite their aversion to anything too serious or overly academic, I always maintained a level of respect for them. All things considered, they were mostly a joy to teach. I also had the added benefit of teaching in my bare feet all day which, apart from the eternally wet bathroom floors, was very comfortable.

This cultural immersion among the monks, living with them and teaching them, exposed me to certain truths. Like all groups of people, some monks are good and some are bad. My previous notion that monks are pious and extraordinarily disciplined men was recalculated on a daily basis.

The temple class for the village children was a different experience from that of the monastic students. Thai children in rural schools are much less likely to encounter a foreigner in the village, much less so in front of the classroom. For this reason alone, there was a palpable energy. The turnout couldn't have been better on our first evening. A total of forty-two endemically, but delightfully bashful, children were in attendance. The temple has several large buildings where classes are held. Our classroom was equipped with desks, fans, and a slightly battered white board. Phra Suwatt and I greeted the kids as they sheepishly entered the room. At one point, we looked at each other in disbelief and I remember thinking, "How am I going to teach all these kids?" I couldn't honestly say that I was qualified to teach anything other than music, much less teach English as a second language to over forty wide-eyed and overly excited Thai kids whose ages and skill levels varied dramatically. I did, however, have a few tools I used as a teacher in the United States that seldom failed me: enthusiasm and creativity.

Most of the kids in the temple English class come from the local village. The village, a small community consisting primarily of farmers, sits snugly abutted along the back wall of the temple. In terms of its economy, it is far from the poorest village in Isan. Like most villages, the houses consist of either traditionally raised teakwood houses or randomly placed concrete block homes, which are essentially unpainted, concrete boxes with a single door and a few simple windows.

In the countryside Thai children can be incredibly shy and a bit fearful of foreign teachers. Going to the front of the packed classroom, I introduced myself. I then went around to each student and asked his or her name. As I did this, I continually introduced myself and offered my hand. Most of the students simply shrank into their seats, while others laughed and screamed encouragement, "Shake hand! Shake hand!"

I've been told that when teaching Thai children, it's important to keep things light and entertaining, and that expressing too much impatience or raising one's voice is not very effective. From what I understand, this is related to a Thai social characteristic of avoiding conflict or tension.

With this always in the back of my mind and a goofy smile on my face, I tried to maintain my classes in the temple by keeping things as interesting and light as possible. I successfully made use of props. A Buddhist temple has a lot of interesting things lying about such as ornate bowls, buckets of colorfully wrapped food items, and all sorts of other sundries. After I dragged these props into the classroom, the class worked together to identify and label them, turning it into a lively game. All things considered, I think it went pretty well.

Getting the monks' classes up and running was difficult. Phra Maha was supposed to be facilitating this class but had yet to announce a date of commencement. He seemed more interested in my driving ability than my teaching ability. Prior to my arrival at the temple, the monks had to hire a driver from the village if they wanted to go anywhere. Soon after my arrival, I found myself in the role of village driver.

Phra Maha is used to people serving him. The temple boys cleaned his cell and girls from the village washed his dishes that he left outside his cell. Not a bad life for a monk. I once remarked to him, "I want to be a monk so I can have beautiful girls fawn over me." He responded, without the least bit of modesty, "You can, Ajarn Bill, you can."

Most of my work as a temple chauffeur was under the pretense of "working on his thesis." At first, this involved driving Phra Maha to MCU to confer with his instructors, but it slowly evolved into frequent and stressful sojourns into Khorat, a city I grew to loathe beyond words. Our destination in Khorat was often the computer mall. I always felt very odd walking with Phra Maha into these types of places. I never imagined I would be shopping for software with a monk.

10

Evenings in the temple were my favorite times. The villagers went home, the dogs were quiet, at least for a little while, and the temple became the peaceful refuge that I longed for.

Wandering the grounds, I smelled the earthy sweetness of melting wax drifting from softly lit windows as it mingled with the scent of the pungent and moist soil. Walking past the bathhouse, I heard the sound of water on concrete and the hollow, muffled sound of a plastic bucket as it slipped in and out of a stained and calcified concrete cistern. In the distance, rusty and tired hinges groaned as collapsing metal doors slammed violently against concrete footings. Geckos and frogs darted clumsily across the darkened path.

As I walked along the gravel main road, the temple dogs, which still terrified me, growled from under a blanket of dark shadows and charged at me in a mock attack. Stomping my foot the way Phra Suwatt would, I made them flee back into their feral fold. Continuing on, I passed Abbot Sunthorn's darkened quarters. After his quarters, I passed by the sala and reached the crematorium, which had become my thinking place.

Funerals are traditionally held inside the temples, and every temple has a crematorium. Some are small and wood-fired while others, like ours, are gas-fueled behemoths. It was a beautiful building and excessively ornate. The eaves dripped with gilded flames and lotus motifs. Wisps of telltale soot streaked upwards from the vents on the stark, white walls. Surprisingly, there was no odor of the previously incinerated. I can't think of a better place to be reminded of the impermanence of life.

I sat upon the cool marble stairway in front of the furnace doors. The stairway, which had been blackened by the dearly beloved, blended eerily into the night. Gazing at the stars, I imagined I could be anywhere and, quietly laughing, reminded myself where I was.

I was not lonely there and this struck me as odd. In the United States, I was often anxious and subject to mild bouts of depression. My nails, which I had habitually bitten for most of my life, had grown back.

Aside from the things that were at first very challenging, the experience was much the life of concentration I desired. I had more time to myself than I had ever had in my life. The extreme polarity of this life from the one I had in the States was exactly what I needed.

As a foreigner, I found myself reflecting on the person I was in the United States and comparing him to this person I was just now getting to know.

I was elated that everything I owned fit into a backpack. My debt was limited to three thousand dollars of revolving credit on a credit card that I could use for escape money if needed. It's no wonder that I could actually meditate now with far greater results. I had very little on my mind. I'm realistic enough to know that I had more to learn, but this was a good start.

My meditation practice had reached a new level. My mind was now less active at the beginning of my meditation. Previously, I spent the better part of an hour trying to settle the stream of thoughts. I reminded myself that the true test would be what happened after I left the temple.

When I first arrived, I thought about leaving almost every day. Evenings were the hardest to cope with when I sat alone in my cell. I no longer had the same longings for home as I did previously. Nevertheless, I found myself occasionally daydreaming about cool sheets, hot showers, and because I was temporarily celibate, all kinds of sordid sexual activity that I must admit involved mostly Thai women.

I often wondered how monks and people in the clergy cope with vows of celibacy. Sexuality is a powerful human condition. I believe that taking a break from sex and getting in touch with what drives us can be healthy, but I'm not convinced that celibacy, as a chosen lifestyle or religious obligation, improves one's spirituality.

I knew that I couldn't conceive of myself living there for more than a year. Westerners just aren't cut out for places like that. Maybe if I were living in a Bangkok temple I would see things differently.

For many of the monks, temple life represents a standard of living that is unattainable in their villages. They have an acute appreciation for what I see as a fairly poor standard of living. Phra Suwatt is a shining example of this. Wat Pramuenrat wasn't simply an escape from the abject poverty of his village but a comparative oasis of comfort and opportunity. I had the honor of going to his village and seeing firsthand where he came from and how his life could have played out had he stayed.

His family, and most of the population in his village, weaves baskets by hand. Although they are intended for everyday use, the baskets are marvels of craftsmanship. One day, while driving around Khorat with Phra Suwatt, I expressed an interest in a local basket shop that had a roadside display. Sitting next to me in the front seat, Phra Suwatt slowly shook his head and said to me, "Ajarn Bill, those baskets come from my village, and they raise price too much. If you want baskets, tell me how much and my family makes for you."

"Really?" I asked. "You mean your family makes those baskets?"

"Yes, my whole village famous for baskets. Everybody makes them—my mother, sister, and many people make all day to sell. How many do you like?"

"Well, I don't really know," I answered, thoughtfully. "I think some small ones would make nice gifts when I go home."

"Okay," he said. "My grandmother can make sticky rice baskets, even small one. Ajarn Bill, we can go to my village and see."

"That would be great. I would love to meet your family." I thought for a moment before I carefully asked, "Phra Suwatt, how long has it been since you've been home to see your parents?"

Looking off into the distance, as if remembering a family meal or his smiling mother's face, Phra Suwatt responded, "Last year ago they come and see me. I tell them not to come now. It's too far." Smiling and looking directly into my eyes, he continued, "Ajarn Bill, I stay now for seven years at Wat Pramuenrat. I go to school in the university and have the good life." It struck me that he recounted this without a hint of regret or melancholy. He seemed to be stating the facts that, in the face of poverty, this is what had to be done. It was neither extraordinary nor worth lamenting over. Over and over, I saw this placid acceptance of the hardships of poverty in the faces of many Isan people.

Listening to this smiling young monk, who spent his adolescent and prime adult years in a dusty, hot temple far from his family, I was reminded of how different I was and what little understanding I had of him. I constantly told myself to be humble, not think of myself, or behave as though I were better than they were.

A few weeks later, we hired a driver from the village and made the four-hour, bone-jarring trip. Distorted house music blared from the pickup truck's cheap speakers as we careened around and over random potholes. We also vaporized a rooster that stood stock still in the middle of the roadway. The driver plowed into it with a dull, wet thud without batting an eye. No one looked back. Under normal circumstances, I would have said something or made some sort of comment, but I thought better of it after reasoning that the rooster probably had bad karma.

Phra Suwatt's village resembled any other poor northern farming community consisting of aged teak houses and ramshackle shops. In the heat of the day there is a heavy stillness that clings to the air, punctuated only by the occasional dove call or chicken cluck. The only remarkable feature of his village were the enormous clusters of handmade baskets in various stages of construction—stacked, scattered, and hung on the undersides of houses. Among their wares, ancient Thai women squatted, weaving, chopping, and cleaving piles of raw materials into meticulously crafted basketry.

When I met Phra Suwatt's parents, they were standing in front of a small, elevated shack that reminded me of chicken coops you might see on an American farm. This was where Phra Suwatt had grown up and where his parents, younger brother and sister live.

Phra Suwatt's perpetually smiling mother prepared a delicious lunch of som tum, curry, and sticky rice. There was also a bowl of bees that they deftly pulled the papery wings from before eating. His father, who was either too shy or busy to join us, spent the afternoon watering the dirt yard with a leaky hose. I felt like a real asshole sitting there with my camera waiting for a good shot.

Phra Suwatt didn't say much at all during lunch and seemed rather sad. I couldn't tell from what little conversation he had with his parents, but something in their demeanor suggested they were not pleased he brought me along. I suspected they were deeply shamed by my presence.

After the meal, for which I expressed my extreme gratitude, his mother brought out a selection of baskets for me to choose from. The craftsmanship was so fine that I asked his mother if she would sign them for me. Everyone thought this was a very strange idea. Embarrassed, she finally agreed. I tried to explain to Phra Suwatt that I viewed the baskets as works of art. To them, however, the baskets were not a creative expression but were everyday tools of survival meant for carrying bits of rice or trapping a fish for dinner.

Feeling more like an asshole with every passing moment, I bought as many as I could and we got the hell out of there. During the ride home, we were silent. I wanted to talk about it, but I knew there was nothing I could say. Except for being born in the United States, the land of opportunity, I didn't do anything wrong that day. I don't know what Phra Suwatt expected by bringing me to his village. Maybe it was just a sales call, but whatever the case, it may have merely served as a reminder to his father that no matter how much he waters the dirt yard, it will always remain just that, a dirt yard.

11

The rainy season was over. No more ants in my rice, no more ants in my coffee, and no more muddy, stinking dogs leaving tracks on my porch. It was also very quiet now in my end of the wat. The neighboring building, which used to bustle with activity, was empty. The monsoon monks who lived there shed their orange robes, put on their counterfeit Levis, and went home. In some ways I was happy because, for a bunch of monks, they were as loud as college students living in a dorm.

The rainy season is traditionally the time when males, aged eighteen and older, go into the temples. Their lengths of stay range from a few days, to a few weeks, and up to the full three months of the monsoon season, hence the term "monsoon monk." These monks attend classes on meditation, scripture, and Pali language, and at the designated time, become ordained as monks for those who qualify. This ordination, or rite of passage, is a time for them to prepare for adult life and marriage.

Concluding their monastic duties, the monsoon monks leave the temple and return to the warmth of their families, sleep in their own beds, and resume whatever sexual relationships, if any, they had waiting for them. This made me a little jealous and very homesick.

It's moments like these, when your mind starts up in that gear you know you have no business driving in, that are the hardest. It was even more difficult because I really had no one I could talk to. Phra Samboen was great and really the best friend I had there, but we are very different people, and not just from a cultural standpoint. Our life experiences have been on two completely different planes. How could I explain to him that sometimes I want my house and old life back? That I want to come home after a long night of playing music at a club and see my girlfriend curled up in my bed with her long, black hair spilling over my pillow? Phra Samboen has never had any of these things. He has been a monk since he had reached puberty, and his family's house in Cambodia is probably smaller than my bedroom. But this is the challenge I wanted. How could I possibly learn anything by lamenting? The truth is it was too late. I couldn't return to my former life and put things back the way they were, even if I tried. Too much had changed.

In a place like this, you find yourself constantly comparing your previous experiences or how it is in the West. This made me realize how much work I had ahead of me and how different I was from those people. I was a ridiculous person. I was beginning to hate myself.

The Dalai Lama suggests when you wake up, look into the mirror and say, "Good morning, not-self." I tried to remember that every day. Unfortunately, I found living there too stimulating. Everything was too new and completely different from anything I had ever experienced. How does one remove oneself from the equation in such a place?

I had become aware of how American I am, and this was a revelation for me. I always considered myself to be worldly and open-minded. Here, I was not. In the space and time I occupied at that moment, I constantly questioned what I should accept, and constantly made comparisons when there was no need to do so. I had so much to learn.

There was an old monk there whom I never saw smile. I often watched him from afar as he delicately swept up around the temple. He did this a lot, and watching him had become a meditation for me. He was old, but he moved with youthful grace and confidence. His thin arms flowed from his robes like brown vines, and his weathered hands grasped the bamboo broom with practiced assuredness. He worked his broom without haste and not a bit of flotsam or debris escaped his concentration.

Unlike the other old monks, he did not smoke. He seldom spoke but when he did, he spoke few words. I passed by the sweeping monk every day and despite the number of times I greeted him, he rarely responded. One day, I think he raised one shaven eyebrow and promptly went back to his work. I didn't know his name, but I'll bet that's fine with him.

He didn't stumble upon his knowledge, and he didn't attain his wisdom by traveling or seeking answers outside of himself. His "self" is nothing like mine. This tortured me because I wanted some of what he knew, but even if he were to share some of his wisdom, I was probably too ignorant and full of myself to absorb much of it. This kind of knowledge must be prospected and discovered within us. It must be done with sacrifice and without complaint. It would require more than a single year in a foreign temple.

Watching him, I wondered if religion is something you follow or are included in, like a flock or congregation. Is spirituality something we feel on an individual level? Is it possible to have one and not the other?

Coming from a devoutly Catholic family, my life was heavily influenced by religion. As a child, I attended Catholic school and Mass every Sunday and confession at least once a month. I can still vividly recall most of my confessions, which consisted of the same three or four sins, and how I used to change them up in case I had the same priest two times in a row.

While Catholicism was a big part of my life, it wasn't a big part of *me*. As a religion, it failed to move me. I'm thankful that I had the blessing of some beautiful and deeply spiritual people in my life. One truly remarkable person, my aunt Sister Mary Delores, was responsible for my earliest experiences regarding spirituality. When I was a boy, her mere presence affected me in a deep and profoundly loving way.

Even though I felt disconnected from the Catholic Church, the way she spoke and carried herself, and, in a word, her *spirituality* made an impact upon me. When I was a young, divorced, single parent, her loving counsel helped me through some very rough periods.

After decades of selflessness, Sister Mary Delores was stricken with cancer and she spent the last of her days in a convent hospital. In these moments of infirmity she did not wear her habit, and for the first time in my life, I could look at her without the ring of starched blue and white around her face. I saw a suffering woman who, steadfast in her belief, was in a state of ecstatic anticipation of her own death. If she was in agony, it was overpowered by her longing for the relief of death.

I'll never forget those moments at her bedside, how beautiful and childlike her face was. She was like a young girl beaming with innocence. To this day I remember how she smiled, and as I huddled closer to the edge of her bed, she said with joy, "Oh! I cannot wait much longer. I'm so tired of living. Pray for me that I will be gone soon." I did.

After she passed, the family was allowed to enter the room she had occupied in the convent. It was suggested that each of us choose an item from among her possessions to remember her by. I looked around the room at the bleak furnishings—an institutional chair upholstered in orange burlap, beige curtains, and a single, narrow bed. I remember thinking that no lover had ever laughed with her or held her closely. Only her pillow caressed her face. Only a crucifix knew of her darkest hours or heard her cries. On the center of the bed, sitting on top of an institutional yellow blanket, was the most beautiful thing in the room—a single grey shoebox that contained her life's possessions.

12

I arrived in Thailand on a thirty day tourist visa. In order to extend my stay I would have to leave the country, if even just for a few hours, and then cross back over the border with another thirty day stamp in my passport.

Rising early the next morning, I headed into Khorat and boarded a third class train to Udorn Thani, the nearest stop to Nong Kia, which is adjacent to the Mekong River, a natural border between Laos and Thailand. From there, I would cross the "Friendship Bridge" into Laos.

If you can handle wooden bench seating, a third class train is the best way to see the country. Unlike first and second class, third class trains stop at every station, and the train seldom gets up to speed before you are jerked away from a daydream. In an attempt to use every available inch of land, the rice paddies sit flush against the train tracks. As the train lumbers along, farmers look up from their rice fields to wave and smile at the passengers. Water buffaloes, black and slick, stare indifferently from cool mud holes. Storybook stations are festooned with flowers, a contrast to the broken concrete benches.

Leathery, old farmers, their heads wrapped tightly in colorful Isan silk, shuffle along the platform. Languishing in the heat, they carry the fruits of their labor and, assisted by other passengers, heave their perishable luggage aboard while grunting in approval. Food vendors travel between stops and trudge the length of the cars, hawking dried squid on a stick, fruit, thick rods of yellow sugar cane, and tepid cans of beer.

To the average country-dwelling Thai, seeing a Westerner on board a third class train is not the norm. On the train, giggling old ladies offered me sticky rice, which I accepted, and dried fish, which I declined. I love the sticky rice, or "kow neaow," which is a northeastern specialty and accompanies every meal. This is rolled into a ball and dipped into a variety of sauces.

Laos is devastatingly poor and third world. After crossing the Friendship Bridge, I waited among a group of French tourists for my passport to clear customs. Oddly enough, I felt more foreign standing around the French than the Thais.

In third world countries I tend to distrust the lower tiers of transportation choices that typically operate without meters. The only exception being the motorcycle taxis in Thailand. Unfortunately, there aren't many conventional taxis in Laos. Ignoring the touts, I chose the least of the bashed-up compacts queued up along the curb. After a bit of haggling, I was off to the capitol city of Vientiane. Getting off at the Thai Embassy, where there was bound to be a selection of accommodations, I looked around the area for a suitable guesthouse. My only real requirement: a hot shower.

After making a few inspections, I chose a quaint guesthouse off a dusty alley that was run by a Frenchmen and his Lao wife. Tucked neatly away from the main road, the house was a traditional Lao dwelling constructed of teak and similar to traditional Thai housing. It was clean and had modern bathrooms, a much-appreciated amenity. I took a single room and had a long and unfortunately cold shower. I had no idea how filthy I was until I saw the black water cascading down the drain. I had to scrub the ground-in dirt from my feet which were calloused from walking in the temple. Feeling newly born and very hungry, I strolled into town in search of food.

Because Laos is a former French colony, it isn't uncommon to see a lone glass bakery case filled with virginal white wedding cakes sitting along an otherwise bleak and dusty street. I was on the prowl for crusty, French loaves when I unexpectedly came upon an Indian restaurant. I nearly fell to my knees with joy. I have a particular love for all Indian food. In the United States, my son and I would often go to our favorite Indian restaurant for the Sunday buffet. I wished he were here. I stood for a few moments as I composed myself while gazing with disbelief upon the faded yellow sign. Yes, I confirmed, it was an Indian restaurant.

When eating abroad, it is generally a good idea to eat at a venue where you see other people. If the locals are eating the food, it is probably a good bet. Even though there wasn't a soul in this place, it was an opportunity I simply couldn't pass up. After being seated by a dour and rather hateful looking waiter, I ordered a combination masala plate and a Kingfisher beer, which I relished. I gazed out on the bustle of the street bronzed by the setting sun.

As I sat, lulled by the street traffic flowing mercilessly by the open door, a tall Lao girl appeared in the doorway. Momentarily blocking out the sun, she leaned casually against the doorframe, flashing me a flirtatious smile. I was bewildered for a moment before she turned away giggling and strutted off as the click of her high feels faded away down the street.

I'm aware of the sex trade in Asia so I wasn't surprised. In fact, I was slightly flattered. I was surprised when, a few a moments later, she came into the restaurant, boldly sat down next to me, and commenced to covertly grope me under the table.

"Hello you," she said. "I very hungry. Can I eat, too?"

"What? Uh..." I stammered.

At this untimely moment, my food arrived and while my waiter gave no verbal opinion of the scene, his expression turned murderous. Perplexed and innocent, which I was, I shrugged and gave him my best, "What? I was just sitting here," expression that I could muster. The girl took no notice of him and unabashedly continued her sales pitch. "I so hungry. I want to eat. Come on, baby." The staff retreated from the dining room and spoke in hushed voices from the kitchen. It was then that I began to imagine myself seated under a flickering bare light bulb at the local police dungeon explaining how much I loved Indian food.

Squeezing a twenty baht note into her free hand, I asked her to go eat somewhere else. Batting her grossly overly made-up eyes, she got up and strutted out as confidently as she had entered, but not before turning to shoot a pouted mouth at me and a real killer of a sneer at the waiter.

Finishing my meal, I quickly paid my bill and hoofed it back through the dusty streets to my guesthouse for another cold shower and a good night's sleep.

The next morning, I headed back over the border with another month of Thai freedom stamped onto my passport. Hurray for small victories.

13

Arriving triumphantly back at the temple, I suddenly realized how different my life had become. Rounding the bend in the gravel road from the main gate and passing the lake, the crematorium loomed slowly into view and I suddenly noticed how quiet it was in the temple. A few of the older monks sat lazing under the pavilion next to Luang Por's cell. As I walked by, they greeted me with soft grunts as they peeked from behind wrinkled newspapers. I looked briefly into Phra Suwatt's cell. As I did, one of the older monks happened to walk by and said, "Monk go today." I thanked him and continued on to my cell.

Seeing random sandals around the temple in all manner of places is not uncommon, so I wasn't at all surprised when I stepped onto my porch to find a pink distressed pair strewn carelessly about the floor. The real surprise was inside.

I don't know how many times I had been told to do this, but I just didn't care enough to lock my cell. I made an exception at night because my cell was along an easy access wall bordering the village. During the day, I never locked it; I just refused to believe anyone would steal anything from a temple. I was attempting, in my own way, to have a certain detachment from my possessions. I had already parted with ninety-nine percent of my life, and if someone was willing to steal whatever I had left, they were welcome to it.

Kicking the sandals aside, I pushed my way inside my cell where I was met with the cool and sharp sensation of glass shards under my bare feet. This was followed by the sound of a piece of glass sliding across the floor after I inadvertently kicked it with my other bare foot. I watched it as it slid, lodging snugly under the refrigerator where it would remain until the end of time.

Setting my bag down near my reading table, I saw the rest of the broken glass that was formerly a small blue and white floral vase. The single yellow and mostly brown flower, its only resident, lay in a beam of dusty sunlight near the window. On the low table, exactly in the same space the vase formerly occupied, was a half-eaten, shriveled red apple (no doubt one of mine) and an empty, half-crumpled drink box of mixed-fruits yogurt. There was also a rather mysterious fist-sized hole in my window screen. This was mysterious because my windows are all heavily barred and welded onto the building. A person would need the Jaws of Life to get in or out of this cell. A fire trap it is, yes, but a very secure one.

Everything else in the cell seemed undisturbed. I then noticed the leg. Picking the glass out of my calloused feet, I happened to look up and from under my mosquito net, see a tawny leg reveal itself, flex diminutive soiled toes, and come to a rest. At first, I stood in a state of shock, which was followed by a mental litany of the possible reasons this leg was in my cell and what excuses I would need if anyone discovered such a leg in my cell, not to mention the other less leggy parts attached to it.

Completely forgetting the fact that I had glass in my foot, I quietly hobbled over to the end of the bed and reached the point where it was possible to peer through the blue translucent netting hanging haphazardly from the ceiling. Curled quite comfortably within a swirling mass of black hair was a partially dressed Thai girl. Her jeans were tossed against the wall and a small pair of pink wire-framed glasses rested in the jumbled folds.

Pacing a few times the length of my cell, I decided I couldn't just wake her up. What if she screamed? I instead decided to go next door to Phra Maha's cell and simply explain to him that I found a sleeping young Thai girl in my bed, and I didn't put her there. He would know what to do. Phra Maha, of course, wasn't there, which was probably a good thing.

Returning, I decided to wake her up and very gently tell her to get the hell out. Thankfully, I know enough about Thai girls to know that touching a female you don't know, and in some cases, even ones you do know, is considered impolite. Keeping a safe distance so as not to startle her, I called out as gently as I could, "Sawat dee." Suddenly, as if attached by a coiled spring, she shot upward from the covers, danced a jig into her jeans, bolted past me and out the door, and jumped the outer wall like a gazelle. On the porch lay a single, faded pink sandal.

Later that afternoon, I saw Phra Maha, who I thought had left with the other monks, emerge sleepy-eyed from his cell.

"Oh, hi, Phra Maha. I thought you were gone."

"Oh, Ajarn Bill, I am too busy working on my master's thesis to go anywhere, and, Ajarn Bill," he said, laughing softly, "I thought you were in Laos today. Why are you here?"

"I was in Laos, but only for a night," I replied. "Phra Maha, ah..."

"When did you arrive in temple?" he said, interrupting me.

"Yeah, that's what I was going to tell you. When I came back this morning, ah... there was a girl in my cell. I didn't know what else to do so I woke her up, which I think really scared her. She ran out and jumped over the wall behind my cell, leaving her glasses and one of her sandals."

"Oh," he said, amused. "It's okay. She is my niece. She came to see me last night and since you were gone, I told her she could sleep in your cell. I'm sorry," he said, laughing. "You must have been very surprised."

"Yeah, a little," I said.

"When I see her, I will tell her to come see you and apologize."

"Yeah, it's no big deal. I'm sure she didn't expect to see me. Okay, well, why don't I just give you her glasses and you can return them to her."

"Of course, Ajarn Bill, for your happiness."

When I ran into sleepyhead Phra Maha emerging from his lair, I was on my way to the sala to meditate. I don't normally meditate there but with everyone gone, it would be quieter than normal and much cooler than walking outdoors behind the crematorium.

The sala is where the meditation programs are held and where the monks meet each morning for chanting and meditation before heading out into the dawn for alms. Inside, along the entire circumference of the towering walls, is a complete hand-painted rendition of the Buddha's life. The end of his life is depicted on the wall behind the main Buddha images. Our temple has three: a large Buddha in the center, flanked by two slightly smaller ones. On the wall above and around their heads, seated Buddha soar through a starry cosmos rising into heavenly enlightenment. As a monk, I often found myself gazing upon this scene with wonderment. Is it really possible to breathe one's way into happiness?

Beginning my meditation, I tried to calm the dynamo in my head. I watched as it spun without my help, tilting and burning with endless mediocre pursuits. It dragged me along as it plowed infertile fields, fields that stretched out like hungry arteries in my mind. Searching and insatiable, breathing in, I was aware that my breath was shallow; breathing out, I was aware that my breath was weak. Relaxing my shoulders, my breathing was lengthened and then distracted. I was aware that I was not aware. I began to think how a person could sit so still and yet have so much chaos within. I imagined that I should be trembling but I was not, and then, like the inside of cool stone, my mind was quiet.

I desperately wanted to change certain things about myself. I recognized that there were things I needed to cast away, things that maybe kept me from enjoying and living my life fully. The death of a loved one has a way of doing that to a person. I miss my mother. She died too young, after a lifelong battle with diabetes. As a child, I remember how, with loving insight, she taught me and my brothers and sisters how to cook and do simple things like laundry and cleaning so that we could take care of ourselves. These were skills I used with great success as a young, single parent.

A spiritual guru of sorts, she extolled the virtues of living in the moment, seizing life, and relying upon a higher power. I wondered what she would say if she could see me in the temple.

My father died a few months before I left for Thailand. He was sick for so long that in the end, his death was a relief. I felt guilty because I remembered feeling glad that I no longer had to go to the retirement facility and watch him drool as he struggled to maintain a place within reality.

My father and I weren't especially close. He was the sort of person who was happier when he was alone with his thoughts. As a mechanical engineer, this often involved eccentric personal projects like the summer he spent building an elaborate squirrel-proof bird feeder. After my parents divorced, he moved back with his parents and from what I can remember, spent the rest of his life lamenting over the loss of his marriage. Because he was Catholic, he never took off his ring. He didn't have any friends, and to my knowledge, he never had a lover.

I can't say he was a very good father. It's my opinion that he squandered his life because he was afraid and in so much pain. As I mourn his passing, I am slowly finding the ability to forgive him. My father was not a loving man, but he was a kind and charitable person who supported Catholic missions and various other charities. He had done his best and whether he knew it or not, taught me a lot about living.

I miss my son terribly. Leaving that life behind was the hardest thing about being in Thailand. My life was inextricably connected with his. To me, leaving him behind was more painful than death. It was also a tremendous source of guilt because I know how badly he wanted me to stay. It killed me to get on the plane with his wet tears still on my collar.

14

Word seemed to be traveling quickly that the wat was offering free English lessons. The student roster for Saturday classes swelled every week, and despite the fact the class was too large to begin with, I couldn't bear to turn anyone away.

Along with the new students who showed up the night of class, there was also an influx of students interested in private lessons. All of these, without exception, had been middle-aged, single women. It's fair to say, and without flattering myself, the majority of them had little to no interest in actually studying English. What they were really interested in was more likely a husband, or at the very least, a boyfriend.

When taking part in any temple program, one must consult with the Abbot, not only to show respect, but also for him to more or less size you up. Needless to say, not one of the several women who came to Wat Pramuenrat for "private lessons," made it past him.

The most memorable case was the day two strikingly beautiful Thai girls came to inquire about the class. We had just finished lunch and everyone was relaxing when we saw them enter the outdoor pavilion. It was obvious to everyone that these were not simple village girls. Noticing them lingering about the pavilion, Abbot Sunthorn calmly packed a fresh slug of beetle nut into his cheeks and, with a grunt, got up to investigate. On the lunch mat the other monks and I looked on as the young women attempted to sit humbly in their incredibly tight jeans. It's easy to forget that these chaste men are monks, nevertheless, it wasn't long before comments regarding the appearance of the girls began to fly.

"Oh! Ajarn Bill, beautiful Thai girl want English lesson with you."

"Hmm... very beautiful Thai girl. You like?"

"Ajarn, how do you feel?"

While sitting with Luang Por, one of the girls even had the nerve to wink at me. It didn't take long for Luang Por to make his assessment. With the expeditious departure of the now pouting Thai women, Luang Por, nearly trembling with laughter, returned to the mat, took a pair of scissors from his basket of beetle nut, and gestured the removal of manhood. This set off great howls of laughter.

"Ajarn Bill," said Phra Suwatt. "They are not good Thai girls so he sent them away. How you feel?" he said, shaking with laughter.

"Tell Luang Por I think he wants me to marry an old woman with no teeth."

This event was recounted with frequency over the next few

days and always brought tremendous laughter whenever it was retold.

In Bangkok, it's not uncommon to see a pudgy middle-aged White guy with a twenty-year-old Thai girl in sprayed-on jeans. That said, though, age does not typically factor into relationships in Thailand the way it does in the United Sates. This, no doubt, has a lot to do with the predominance of older, and often incredibly unfit, Western men who have Thai girlfriends or wives.

People, including some of the monks, frequently ask me why I don't have a Thai girl. "Every foreign man have Thai girl. Why you not have? You want be with boy?" But alas, I didn't go to Thailand for Thai women (or men for that matter). I came here to meditate in a temple and be a teacher.

Not all men that come to Thailand do so for the women— although it is likely that many have stayed for that very reason. The majority come to teach English. Not only is it one of the few ways a foreigner can legally stay in the country, but also a great way to learn about an extraordinary culture.

The teaching options here are plentiful. So much so that anyone, provided they're not a complete idiot, can literally get off the plane and find work in a very short time.

I've taught in several institutions, and while I retain a profound appreciation for my life here, teaching in this country leaves much to be desired. If there was ever a situation in my life where I had the need for abrupt adaptation, other than the temple, the Thai education system was it.

Cell phones, which have become a sort of weird cultural addiction, constantly rang out during lectures, and if they weren't ringing, it was because the students were carrying on deep and meaningful conversations via text messaging. Cheating, a real art form here, takes place on a comical scale. I once had an entire class of twenty-eight students turn in the exact same paper printed directly from a website. Unfortunately for them, the website, and consequently every single assignment handed in to me, was in the French. *Ah Non!*

Many teaching opportunities in Thailand can be found in private language schools, which have spread at an alarming rate throughout the country. These institutions can be a fair option for new teachers or those with limited credentials. Besides the language schools, there are also government university positions. These pay a bit less than the mostly profit-driven language schools, but include the added benefit of health insurance and greater ease in obtaining the coveted one-year visa and work permit. They are also completely legal, allowing a person to stay in the country almost indefinitely as long as he or she is employed.

The visa situation in Thailand is severely bureaucratic. I've just as many good experiences as I have bad experiences. It isn't terribly uncommon for people to live and work here illegally for months and sometimes years. I could probably spend the rest of my life in Isan and no one would be the wiser. The penalty for overstays is pretty clear, though, and could easily result in instant deportation and refused future entry. I have heard and read of a few cases where it sometimes resulted in lengthy imprisonment, courtesy of the Thai penal system.

Teachers employed through bona fide institutions typically have few problems obtaining visas. Because I was technically a volunteer, I, on the other hand, fell into a grey area. Although there was some hope the temple would be able to eventually host my visa, I, in the meantime, faced numerous and expensive trips to Laos in what's known as a "border run."

In my case, a border run entailed leaving the country by crossing into Laos. Cambodia and Burma, depending on the location, are also suitable re-entry points. Upon re-entry into Thailand, American passport holders are entitled to an automatic thirty-day tourist stamp.

This is a tactic used by many individuals who either teach illegally or enchanted by life here, refuse to leave. It goes without saying that customs on both ends are most likely aware of this, as the profits are probably tremendous. Having one too many tourist stamps when it's obvious you're basically living in Thailand could very well lead to a refusal at some point.

I would like to be able to return. In fact, I considered never leaving. For this reason, I reluctantly decided to find teaching work in the nearby town of Cho Ho. I didn't exactly want to because I was primarily afraid of being distracted from my temple responsibilities.

Cho Ho, which is located a few miles from the wat, is about as small as a town gets before it's called a village. I stood along the road outside the temple gate and waited for the red and white covered truck to drive by. These have a covered seating area in back, and are one of several options of public transportation. There are also buses, but I've yet to figure them out.

In the countryside, the people are a bit shocked to see me hop onto these. The children on board usually shriek and flee into their mothers' arms, and even though they stare at me as if I were deformed, everyone is very kind and friendly.

In the country there aren't any conventional bus stops. Once in the general area, you simply ring the electric bell, and after hopping off, pay the five-baht fare to the driver. It's an efficient and wholly dependable system of transport that makes getting around incredibly easy once mastered.

Cho Ho, like every town or city in Thailand, has a language school. Typically, these are the easiest options for landing employment because they are frequently in need of teachers. This is especially true in rural areas since most foreigners prefer to work in Bangkok or other more exciting places. It didn't take me long to find the one and only school in Cho Ho, mostly because the whole town stretches the length of roughly three city blocks.

As luck would have it, they were currently seeking a new foreign language teacher. After a brief interview, where I was assured of obtaining the proper visa, they made several copies of my documents, handed me a schedule, and that was that. With schedule in hand, I hopped back on the red-and-white, loosened my tie, and headed back triumphantly to the temple just in time for lunch. Once I was back at the temple, I quickly changed, had a cool bucket bath, and made it to lunch with Luang Por just as the bell rang. Before lunch, I always greet Luang Por with three very respectable bows from the knees. I then sit Thai style with my legs off to the side while being careful not to expose the bottoms of my feet. As always, Phra Suwatt is at lunch with Luang Por. Phra Maha, who is typically late, is also present. We each touch the trays of food as an offering and commence eating.

Retreating off to one side of the mat, I settle down with a Thai newspaper and wait. With his back to me, Phra Maha asks,

"Ajarn Bill, you look very handsome today leaving temple. Where do you go?"

"I'm worried about my visa," I replied, "so I went into Cho Ho to see if I could find a job at a language school."

"Hmm ... and they can?" asked Phra Maha.

"Well, they said they could get me a visa I hope so," I answered.

This was then related to Luang Por who made a few comments between spoonfuls of fish soup.

"Ajarn Bill," continued Phra Maha. "What about your schedule? Luang Por worry you work too much."

I replied, "I'll have to teach fifteen hours a week in order to get a visa. I can do it. Besides, I don't know what else to do. I can't keep going to Laos. I can't afford it."

"I see," answered Phra Maha. "Luang Por say he will try and get visa for you as a special volunteer teacher in the temple, but we never do this so it may take time. He also wants to help you with money."

Pausing to wai Luang Por in gratitude, I shook my head and told Phra Maha that I simply couldn't allow myself to accept any money from the temple. Wide-eyed and laughing, Phra Maha replied, "Ajarn Bill, Luang Por love you and he wants you to stay here a long time. Giving you money is for his happiness; for that you cannot say no."

After lunch, I felt a determination to do whatever was necessary to stay, even if it meant working in Cho Ho. My first commitment, however, was to the wat, and after such an earnest display of warmth from Luang Por, my affection for him had only deepened. I retreated to my cell but feeling too anxious to sit inside, I went out to the garden which I had neglected to water in the morning in my hurried bid for employment. Over the months, I had perfected the design by hauling gravel from the other side of the grounds and transplanting a variety of plants from all around the temple. It was by no means a botanical masterpiece, but it was a far cry from the rubbish dump it once had been.

The main focal point of the garden, which was approximately forty square feet, was a low ceramic vessel of water. These vessels of water, which we had all over the temple, were filled with water and different varieties of lotus. I put a single floating white lotus blossom into mine and carefully anchored it to the bottom with rocks. I also added some tiny goldfish that I netted from similar vessels from all around the temple. The fish are nice to watch as they dart among the lotus and feed upon the mosquito larva.

Much can be said about the simple joys of coaxing life from the earth. The act of planting a garden has become another form of meditation for me. What makes it especially beautiful is that once you've worked the soil through your hands, experiencing its different textures and aroma, and then gently tucked in the plants, you can sit beside the garden and meditate on its simple beauty.

I was rather amazed at my own success, because the only thing I was ever able to grow in the states was a few sickly corn stalks. On the other hand, my father was a talented botanist. He would spend all winter just getting ready for spring. As a child, I often found him in the basement working quietly under florescent lights among rows of delicate seedlings. I wondered if he had been gently directing my spade in his silent way.

If I sat quietly long enough beside my garden, the unseen doves cooing from the treetops dropped down to drink. Snakes to, with which I have had my share of experiences while living here, also became a common sight. They are found in abundance in this part of the country. I have had snakes in my bathroom and on my porch. I even nearly stepped on a very green one while walking among the bamboo by the lake. They didn't frighten me the same way they used too. As they made their way through the underbrush along the wall, I found that it was better to just sit and watch as they slithered through.

The biggest and most unlikely member of this burgeoning ecosystem was discovered the day a very excited novice pounded on my door and hurriedly led me out to a huge snapping turtle, which had parked itself right under my window. It was a long way to the lake, and everyone agreed that it was very strange that the turtle was somehow in the back corner of the grounds. Making a sling from monks' robes, we gently slid it under its belly and carried it off to the lake where it literally hurled itself into the water.

At Wat Pramuenrat, the care of the grounds is primarily done by three old monks who could be seen at almost any moment of the day tilling, watering, or planting around the temple. They even had a wildly overgrown herb garden planted around the lake. Despite the fact that the herbs were grown using lake water, they were delicious and we ate them every day.

The old monks, who lived at the other end of the grounds, seldom watered or tended any of the numerous plots of barren soil in the area where I resided. So, no longer limiting myself to the garden along the back wall where really no one but me ever visited, I began to concentrate on these areas as well. Most of the credit for these other gardens actually belonged to the village children who planted them during a meditation camp.

Taking responsibility for these areas gave me a greater sense of purpose, and now every evening I had something to do besides sitting alone in my cell. After class, when all the chattering monks had retreated to their cells and the laughing squads of children had drifted into the village, I made a steaming glass of instant coffee, slipped on my sandals, and lazily wandered about the grounds in complete solitude.

Inclined to ritual, I always began my watering rounds at the bell tower. Surrounding it, save for a small gap for entering, was a low wall which contains the children's flowers. Like the tower, this was also made of concrete, and judging by the remaining grossly failing paint, used to be white. Despite this, it was absolutely crawling with lotus buds and sprawling petals fashioned in relief. It was magnificent.

While watering at the tower, I was often struck by a black and white photo which was permanently affixed into the masonry. The image, like an old daguerreotype, featured a beautiful young Thai woman. With blazing dark eyes, she peered from its surface; her mouth set, not with a smile, but with an expression of youthful determination. As I watered, her gaze followed and momentarily transfixed me no matter how often I looked upon her.

The monks told me she died twenty years ago. And, in order to earn merit, her family funded the construction of the tower. I wondered about her life and if her family, in a moment of longing, ever came here to gaze upon her cracked and fading likeness as it sank into the surface of this now dilapidated bell tower. I hope she knows that, in a very odd way, she gave me comfort.

Many sleepless nights, I entered the narrow gallery and passed her image to climb the dark spiral staircase leading to the bell house. From this vantage above the canopy, the countryside spread out before me. The spire of the crematorium from behind the sala threaded the sky like an ornate needle, and endless rice paddies faded to black above a star-packed and glittering sky.

15

I found it very odd that whenever I told the monks, especially Phra Maha, that a person frequently jumped over the temple wall late at night, they failed to see the significance. I wonder what they would say if I told them it was a girl.

Again unable to sleep one night, I was standing within the caged porch. Smoking, I gazed languidly at my dog asleep atop a round concrete table. As I cleared my throat, she immediately snapped her head up and cowered in fear. She wasn't the brightest dog, and it took her a moment to recognize me. She immediately hopped down, paused for a vigorous scratching, chewed on something between her legs, and skittered over as her tail flitted nervously in small bursts. I was in no mood to let her in but happily scratched her yellow mud-flecked nose through the bars, cooing and reassuring her. Circling the other doors and crying meekly, she departed to her perch and exhaled a frustrated huff in defeat.

As I listened to the country night, the clouds randomly parted the light of the moon, momentarily brightening the night in metallic shades of blue. I contemplated rounding the darkened corner of my cell to the bathroom, but instead stayed put and aimed through the bars for the garden.

I was preparing for release when, for the second time, a dark figure bolted over the garden wall. I was hidden completely in the shadows but no less startled and still handily, in the literal sense, in relief mode. After landing softly in commando posture, the figure paused. In the moonlight, I saw the unmistakable figure of a girl with her long hair bounding out behind her as she pattered off behind Maha's cell. Not interested in giving chase, I listened for a few moments and after the tension eased, I let my stream fly through the bars. She wasn't there to see me.

The next morning, I arose to the bell in an irritated and restless state. Forgoing my garden constitutional, I instead lay lamely on my mat listening as the village loudspeaker crackled and ignited into its usual litany of distorted ramblings. I didn't want to hear it and wished they would shut up.

That morning, I was overtaken by deep misgivings, homesickness, and the urge to check into the finest hotel I could find in Khorat where I could slip between clean, cool sheets and sleep the whole thing off. Before I could carry this fantasy any further, I heard soft knocking at my door. Not wanting any company, I stared up at the cobwebbed ceiling and wished them away. A few moments went by, but the knocking continued. It was quiet but insistent, and for the love of God, or Buddha, I couldn't imagine who it could be. It couldn't be Phra Maha; he would simply begin calling out my name in his mocking lilt,

"Aaajarn Beill!" Phra Suwat, who is far more considerate, might also call my name but pose it as a carefully and gently phrased question, "Ajarn Bill? Ajarn Bill, you OK?" It could be Phra Samboen, but he hardly knocked loud enough for me to even hear and would typically loiter outside until I happened to see him. Besides, he seldom visited in the morning.

Exasperated, I wrapped my damp bath towel around my bare waist. Venturing out upon my porch, I was aghast to find an entire family standing assuredly in front of my cell. "Oh! Sawat dee kup," I exclaimed. An older woman, no doubt the mother, had in her hands a massive platter, upon which lay an entire stewed duck, its blanched and dripping head swaying listlessly over the edge. I remember thinking, "Oh, well you shouldn't have!"

The others, a man and two teenage girls, peered wide-eyed from behind the relative safety of their duck-toting mother who continued to stare, equally aghast but no less confident. At this point, the man locked his gaze upon me and whispered something to the mother, who then carefully handed him the platter of duck. She slowly and quietly spoke as she smoothed her hands and nodded to the slain duck, and then hopefully into my open cell. Of course, I didn't understand a word of this, but it was clear that the duck, and at least one of them, needed to go inside for some reason. "Oh," I said, as I pointed back into my cell, smiling disarmingly. "You want to come in!" Beaming now with weak smiles of understanding, I ceremoniously outstretched my arms and invited them inside with as much warmth as a half-naked American man in a bath towel could muster.

Standing inside my cell with the now smiling family, and what was probably once the family duck, I was fraught with yet another moment of tension. We all stood there for a moment: me in my bath towel, the duck dripping little brown circles of juice on my floor, and the happy little Thai family. Gathering my clothes in haste in aid of my modesty and nodding assuredly, I retreated to the bathroom to dress and wait them out, duck and all, within the confines of my garden. A few minutes barely passed before they were on their way out the door. Smiling and nodding in gratitude, they made their way down the walkway without the duck. Inside, it immediately became apparent they were relatives paying homage to a deceased member of their family who was sealed behind my walls.

The curtains to the antechamber were pulled open, and upon the concrete ledge, which had been cleared of layers of dust, was smoldering sweet Chinese incense, a shot of clear hard liquor, and finally, the duck. While I was surveying the scene, Phra Suwat strode onto my porch to tell me that a family would come to pay respects and not worry.

The practice of interning the remains of loved ones in temple walls is believed to bring merit to the family. The families not only pay for this service but also for the building in which the remains are kept if the family is wealthy. Most cells here have a random picture or engraved inscription of someone whose family arranged to have their remains placed there; however, my cell is unique in that it has an actual antechamber for this purpose.

For the families of limited means, there is also the option of having a *chedi* placed in the temple, which is a more common practice. Made of concrete and in the typical spiraling Thai motif, these monoliths can be seen in every temple in Thailand. Since I had been in residence, I had seen the addition of three of these, one of which was completely covered in tiny mosaic mirrors and topped off with a golden seated Buddha image. Like the bell tower girl, these sported eerie black and white images of the deceased, which fade over time into mysterious negatives images.

One of the things that struck me about the Thai people was how deeply superstitious they were. Many wouldn't even consider entering the temple after dark because it was a cemetery of sorts. As far as they were concerned, the temple was frequented by wandering spirits, or *phee.* Many people, after learning I lived in a temple, asked with certain amazement if I had seen any *phee.* I could say thankfully that I hadn't.

After the duck family departed, I had to get dressed for my first day of work at the language school in Cho Ho. I can't say I was very excited about this, but since it was the only way I could acquire a visa, I didn't have much choice.

Teachers in Thailand are expected to dress professionally. Putting on my best white oxford shirt that was freshly laundered and expertly pressed by a sweet older village lady, I reluctantly tightened my tie and headed out into the sweltering heat to hail a red-and-white.

Arriving at the school, I was introduced to the staff, who were painfully shy, and then I was given quick tour by the school's owner whom everyone called by the nickname of Pooh. Thai are quite fond of nicknames. They're also quite fond of Winnie the Pooh whose cheerful image in various states of honeyed glee can be seen emblazoned on just about anything from backpacks to busses. I remember once meeting the dean at a government university who was wearing full-on "Whiney the Pooh' dress."

I've been told, and it was certainly the case there, that Thai parents tend to spoil their children. The students at this school could only be described as a unified force of over-developed petulance. The school was nothing more than a glorified day care center, and my experience here turned out to be a mostly regrettable experience.

Ajarn Pooh seemed like a nice enough person but the Thai are not always easy to figure out, especially with all that smiling. It is a social game that I do not know how to play.

After a day of Thai kids and insane "Whiney the Poohs" dancing through my head, I looked forward to getting back to the relative peace of the temple. After waiting for the red-and-white, which was completely jammed with students, I relinquished the extra fifteen-baht for a motorcycle taxi that whisked me away at breakneck speed before dropping me directly in front of Luang Por's cell. As I was peeling myself from the seat, Phra Maha, who was sitting in the shade of the sala, greeted me with his usual enthusiasm.

"Ajarn Bill, how are your students today?"

Completely overheated in my black pants and buttoned-up shirt, I was hoping to retreat to my cell for a cooling bucket bath.

Sitting with Phra Maha was a middle-aged woman who was dressed impeccably in what appeared to be a civil servants uniform. Thai uniforms are difficult to identify accurately, and it seems like everyone has one.

Waving me over before I could escape, Phra Maha said, "Ajarn, please come here and join us. I want you to meet someone."

So, greeting him with a wai and sighing inwardly, I joined them on the mat.

"Phra Maha, how are you today?" I asked, in as a relaxed and carefree a manner as I could manage.

"I am very good, thank you. Today a very important teacher has come to see me, and I want you to talk with her."

At some point during the ensuing conversation, my mind, as well as the lower half of my body, went completely numb. Take my advice and never, under any circumstances, attend any situation involving a Thai official. This includes weddings, funerals (especially funerals), school functions, temple programs, or any other event that features anyone wearing a uniform. And don't let the uniforms intimidate you. The Poo Yai once showed up for a funeral dressed like the admiral of the Pacific fleet.

In the temple, I was often summoned to meet officials from various government ministries. These were torturous and drawn-out affairs that involved a great deal of etiquette and copious kowtowing by the various officials. As a guest, it was a social imperative that I attend some of these meetings. In all honesty, however, I found it exhausting repeating what little Thai I knew in response to the same questions invariably related to Thai food, Thai women, and my origins.

16

It is the mating season and the dogs are out of control. Both day and night, vicious dog fights erupt all over the grounds, as the male dogs brazenly invade neighboring territories in search of females. The level of violence is truly unbelievable. This continued day and night for weeks and made sleep nearly impossible.

The dogs were humping away with abandon all over the temple. Although I found this disturbing, no one else seemed to notice. Monks strolled past these displays of nature without as much as a glance.

The poor females, who had bloody open sores on their haunches, were nearly mated to death. They pumped out litter after litter, further taxing their already malnourished systems. There was the case of one particular female. She was there when I first arrived and was clearly the lowest member of the pack. She was under constant harassment by the others, who routinely prevented her from eating even when I tried to feed her. She was lying in the middle of a walkway on the morning I found her. Her nursing pups had sucked the life right out of her. I wrapped her in the moldy shred of a monk's robe and buried her in a shallow sandy grave. The village kids gathered most of her pups, while those who remained wandered around the temple learning to fend for their lives. I tried to keep an eye out for them, but it wasn't long before they too disappeared.

The dogs that aren't fed outright mostly eat leftover rice and whatever rancid scraps of meat and fish are left over from temple meals. The monks simply dump this in the area behind my bathroom. It is littered with mounds of rotting rice and hundreds of plastic bags. In the rainy season, the rotting rice ferments and replaces the septic stench with an aroma much like sake and body odor.

Despite the oppressive heat, there isn't any fresh water available for the dogs, which, instead, drink from the slimy black gutter or the many stagnant vessels of water. I tried unsuccessfully to put fresh water out for them, but with the exception of my dog, they seemed fearful of the bowls.

I found it disturbing in terms of Buddhist compassion that the people here, including the monks, seemed to ignore the fact that these animals were suffering. Few made any effort to help those who suffered from injuries or starvation. Had this gone on for so long that it reached a point where it was simply accepted?

Since compassion is the cornerstone of Buddhism, I found this very perplexing. I frequently found myself wondering what exactly these people were thinking. They performed so many odd and seemingly mindless acts. Most of these were little things, but they really got under my skin.

I had worked very hard to manage the children's gardens around the bell tower. Every weekend I spent hours weeding and watering and then, without explanation, someone decided it was the perfect place to burn a pile of leaves mixed with plastic bags. They did this all over the temple, piling them around trees and in the middle of concrete walkways. It was as though they simply didn't care.

The monsoon monks, who used to live next door to me and had since gone home, would gather their garbage into a pile against the bell tower. After lighting the pile of garbage on fire at night, they sometimes stood around it like a bunch of hobos dressed in monk's robes. I had to ask myself if it was really alright for a bunch of monks to stand around a pile of smoldering garbage. Okay, I know I'm different. I realize I'm an American. I assure you, it's abundantly clear. But what does it mean? Does it mean that Buddhism, at least in Thailand, is nothing but a ruse? Am I a complete idiot for investing so much energy into going there?

It's dangerous for me to say these things. It's dangerous because I don't want to condemn the whole country or the face of Thai Buddhism, nor can I since this was just one experience in time; nevertheless, I had to wonder about other people's experiences. It seems that everything I read previous to my arrival painted a far different and romantic picture that, quite frankly, I was not able to see.

So much had happened since I got out of that tuk tuk and entered this world. That was a romantic moment. In many ways,

I was still the ignorant American guy living in the temple; except now, I was willing to admit it. And while I like to think there were moments when I was no longer a bystander, and there were moments of purity, those moments were probably my own. The truth is I could have lived there the rest of my life and still die a stranger. It makes little difference how well I sat or conducted myself because there were parts of the picture I would never be able to see.

17

Tonight I have to meet "the great monk" in his cell to begin editing his thesis. It suffices to say my enthusiasm to serve him was seriously lacking. Taking the short walk over to his cell, I entered and was immediately surprised to see an incredibly attractive Thai woman perched behind his cluttered desk. Phra Maha casually introduced her as a childhood friend and former classmate.

"Oh Ajarn Bill, we have been friends for so long. When I was a little boy we went to the same school in my village. She just graduated and is now to help me with my thesis."

Introducing myself, I noticed that her demeanor was reluctant and bashful. Without speaking, she peered over the glow of the computer and offered me a weak smile while cowering down behind the monitor. Then, in very low deliberate tones, Phra Maha said something that drove her away to prepare two glasses of water from his personal water cooler. As is customary, monks are always served first. With a dismissive wave, he declined, but since I now considered cold water a luxury, I gladly accepted and helped myself to another without asking.

Taking in his cell, I noticed that compared to the other monks, Phra Maha lived a life of affluence and comfort. In the very front of his cell, he had a main work area that consisted of his office and a massive altar of dusty, ill-kept Buddha images. He even had a second room. Peeking into this extra room, I was amazed to see it outfitted with a queen-sized bed, TV, stereo, refrigerator, and air conditioning. I also noticed that the entrance to his bathroom was actually indoors. As I finished my third glass of ice cold water, I was further amazed to see his friend casually throw herself upon his bed and begin surfing the web with his laptop. If I had known we could have women in our cells, I would have tried to keep the one I found sleeping in mine.

In the outer office, Phra Maha eagerly invited me to sit next to him at his computer.

"Okay Ajarn, my proposal is finished, and now we can begin the editing. I am so happy you are helping me! I could not do this without you Ajarn. You are the English expert, thank you."

"Maha, thank you, but I'm no expert. I will do whatever I can to help you, though."

"It's OK, Ajarn. You are a native speaker, so to me, you are the expert."

This "edit" turned out to be almost a total re-write. Huge swathes of text screamed plagiarism. At one point, I turned to him and said, "Phra Maha, you can't submit this."

"Ajarn Bill, what do you mean?" he asked, somewhat amazed.

"Well, Maha, you can't use someone else's work, at least not in this magnitude."

Looking rather perplexed, he responded, "That's OK; this is Thailand."

"You mean no one cares?" I asked.

"No one will know or not. I just need you to check the English. It's OK, Ajarn Bill."

"Are you going to try and publish your thesis?" I asked.

"Yes, of course," he replied.

After two very stressful weeks of our late-night sessions, the edit was going nowhere. Eventually, we were both so frustrated that I simply stopped going to his cell altogether. In all honesty, I felt I had more important things to do like preparing and maintaining my classes, not only for the forty-some-odd children but also for the monks' classes.

Phra Maha, in typical Thai grace of avoiding conflict, hardly mentioned his thesis again except when he needed a ride somewhere in support of it. These rides, in turn, increased in frequency. His childhood friend, my replacement, spent more time in his cell and assumed the role of what he referred to as research assistant and secretary for the purposes of its completion. This, of course, resulted in my driving to pick her up from her village and in some cases, to drop Phra Maha off at her home.

Summoning me from his cell window, Phra Maha would put on his game face of the hardworking intellectual and tiredly announce, "Ajarn, we must go to my friend's so I can finish my thesis." Roped in again, I let him hand me the keys through the bars of his window. As instructed, I started the aged van and pulled it directly in front of his cell. Smugly sliding into the back (never in front), he directed me through the back gate and into the darkened village before reaching the main road.

I really hated the temple van. It had virtually no suspension to speak of and despite my best efforts, I managed to hit every pothole, which were so numerous and deep that they momentarily threw us off course. Jerking upon the un-powered wheel, I made my way to the freeway, and with my foot pressed to the spongy floor, I white-knuckled my way into traffic.

As a rule, it's always been my understanding that women are not allowed to closely associate with monks for any reason. In fact, even your own mother, except in cases of extreme illness, is forbidden to embrace or touch you in any way.

At Phra Maha's friend's house, I was forced to enjoy the pleasantries of her dumbstruck family who stared at me transfixed. Sitting on mats in the unpainted concrete living room, I sipped tepid water and pretended to enjoy an inexplicably loud Thai game show featuring pigs and what looked like a giant tub of yogurt. From the other room, no doubt working hard on his thesis, Maha's arrogant laughter grated on what little patience I had left. Exasperated, I excused myself to wait him out in the refuge of the van.

Phra Maha's royal self-image and indolent life continued to mystify me. My respect and admiration, which in the beginning of our relationship were so strong, waned considerably. I noticed the other monks tended to avoid him; in fact, they had a knack for fading away upon his approach. While they congregated together in groups and socialized during meals and other functions, Phra Maha rarely participated. The only monk who had much to do with him, and only because of his position as secretary, was Phra Suwatt; even then, the tension between the two was palpable.

One night, completely fed up and in an effort to evade him, I avoided my cell entirely and went to see Phra Samboen. Taking refuge in his cell, I decided I had to talk to someone about what was going on. It just didn't seem right to me; not only the fact that he was taking advantage of me but also his very unbecoming behavior. Confiding in Phra Samboen I asked him point blank, "Phra Samboen, what do you think of Phra Maha?"

"Ajarn Bill," he said, setting down his coffee, "I know Maha only a little. He does not come here except to tell other monks what to do. Other Thai monks know him more. I cannot say these things because I am Cambodia monk and do not want to be trouble. All Cambodia monks feel this too."

"Well, you know I respect monks, but Phra Maha is always asking me to drive him somewhere and doesn't seem to care that I might be busy doing something else and I'm not here to be his driver or assistant."

"Yes, I think so, Ajarn."

"The problem is how do I say no?"

"Oh... Ajarn Bill, no one says no to Maha. Many times he ask me for help when I am study very hard but since I am Cambodia monk, I do it. Maybe you speak with Phra Suwatt and he talk to Maha."

"Yeah, maybe, I just don't want to cause trouble."

Phra Samboen then leaned in, clasped his robes at his chest, and quietly said, "Every monk know about Maha but no one says. Don't worry, Ajarn Bill."

I felt better after speaking with Phra Samboen, and it was nice to have a night off from Phra Maha. As I descended the worn steps out of the glow of his porch light, I could still hear him: "Every monk know about Phra Maha."

As I entered the folding darkness, I heard the faint rustle of a running animal followed immediately by feeling the cold sensation of teeth sinking into my flesh. I whipped around, grabbed my leg, and stumbled into a stack of red plastic lunch chairs. The biggest bitch of the temple, the most surly and ill-tempered, had just taken a chunk out of my leg.

Instead of fleeing, I began throwing anything I could find, which happened to be the plastic lunch chairs. Stacked conveniently like ammunition, I grabbed them and hurled them blindly into the dark. After the dog's retreat, which was sudden and without so much as a single bark, I went immediately to my cell to inspect my wound. Sunk into my calf were three neat puncture holes. Not having any available first aid I went to see Phra Suwatt for help.

"Ajarn Bill, what happened?" he said, inspecting my wound.

"I was leaving Phra Samboen's cell and one of the dogs by the lake attacked me."

"Oh, very bad dog, Ajarn. We should go to Luang Por so he know about this."

Because I am often subject to Luang Por's odd sense of humor, I exclaimed, "Luang Por sunat mai dee mak mak!" (or "very bad dog") as I pointed to my leg. Looking at my leg and taking in my agitated state, Luang Por began laughing hysterically. Maybe he was surprised I knew that much Thai, but at any rate, he instructed Phra Suwatt to fetch some first aid, which he quickly brought from his cell. This was a good sized plastic box (yellow, of course) and contained a multitude of little glass bottles reminiscent of the 1950s. Locating the iodine by smell, and bleeding so sufficiently that any rabies I might have contracted would bleed out, I cleaned and wrapped my leg in what I hoped was a sterile bandage.

It so happened that the dog that attacked me, like most of the females, had just delivered pups, and while she typically stayed next to the lake, she had made a den under Phra Samboen's cell. I know I should have gone to seek medical attention. Common sense would have mandated a series of rabies shots, but considering that she had pups, her behavior was easily explained.

The next morning, while I was passing by the lake with a suitable length of bamboo in hand, she kept her distance. Other than her obvious disdain for me, she also seemed relatively healthy. Placing my stick in the crook of a tree next to the gate for later use, I exited the temple and waited for the red-and-white. Waiting there, I watched the old monks as they wandered along the road tending the grounds. One of them was smoking a huge hand-rolled cigarette. As I boarded the truck, he looked up and waved goodbye as if he would never see me again.

18

Things were not going quite as well as I'd hoped at the language school. The kids were great at being kids, but very poor at being students. In fits, the worst of them kicked the walls, slammed the doors, and frequently pulled on my clothes. To make matters worse, I think Ajarn Pooh kowtowed to the parents and refused to keep the kids in line to avoid their complaints. The kids pretty much ran the show, and I felt more like a very ineffective baby sitter than a teacher. I hated them.

Oddly, Ajarn Pooh seemed particularly distressed, and even annoyed, about my living at the wat and was not afraid to express this. One day, she looked at me from across her desk and said, "Ajarn, you know monks do not understand the responsibilities of the real world. Their lives are very different from ours. Be careful; you might find yourself working there too much." I nodded my head slowly in agreement. "I think you're right about that, but that's why I'm there."

"Yes, but what about your schedule here? I worry about that."

"I can understand that, Ajarn Pooh, but I can handle both. Anyway, I only teach a few hours at the wat."

"Well, just be careful. Sometimes monks may ask too much."

I felt uneasy about this conversation as Thais generally do not openly criticize. I also think her concern for my time had more to do with her own well-being than it did for mine.

There was such a sharp contrast between her kids and the ones I taught at the wat. Unlike the kids at the language school, the village children seemed to really want to learn, and while there were moments of complete chaos, the students seemed genuinely interested. The classes, although exhausting, were great fun, and the children were so charming that when I think about them, even now, I want to laugh.

The village children became my teachers. They continually showed me that a person such as me could make a difference. Even with such limited experience teaching English, I found myself tapping into a new sense of creativity; a creativity that in the United States had become barren and lackluster. Teaching them forced me to dig deep, and yet it seemed to happen automatically. I somehow stood in front of that packed room every Saturday night, and with ease and confidence, managed to pull together an entire room of smiling children.

The monks, too, had a childlike innocence, and their classes were very similar in terms of energy to that of the children's. It was also easier to teach their much smaller class, which was not quite as chaotic, although they could be quite verbose and had an infectious way of laughing at the simplest things.

Their class, which started out with twelve, was currently in a state of flux as the less serious students dropped out. The only ones remaining were Phra Samboen, the most talkative; four other Cambodia monks; and Phra Suwatt, whose attendance was sporadic due to his responsibilities.

It's interesting that the Khmer monks, who probably came from an even deeper source of poverty than the majority of the Thai monks, were so much better students than the Thais. In my opinion, it was this way because they had something to prove.

The Thai, despite their legendary tolerance, are fiercely nationalistic when it comes to their history with Cambodia. There were private debates among the Khmer monks over what they believed were blatant historical inaccuracies in Thai textbooks, as well as in history lectures at university. In the temple, it was difficult to pick up on this as it was not openly discussed. I noticed that the Khmer monks seemed to live in the same general area and associate mostly within their own group. All of them, without exception, did not have any intention of staying in Thailand after they graduated.

After classes at the language school, I usually went for coffee at a tiny stall in the back of the sprawling wet market. Crossing the street one day, I was visually struck by a giant glittering image of the King of Thailand being hoisted up a concrete bridge pillar. Momentarily impeded by the workers, and indeed the size of the image, I squinted at the curly lettering and took in the magnificent glinting gold and red of His Majesty's waist coat. I watched as the workmen delicately secured the images over the bridge way. Farther round the block on my way to the catch the red-and-white, more images were seen hanging from all manner of available high points in various stages of elevation. The affection the Thais have for their king is not a seasonal or rote tradition. Judging by the preparations leading up to his birthday on the fifth of December, it is an event that is taken very seriously.

His Majesty, King Bhumibol Adulyadej (also known as Rama IX), is the world's longest reigning monarch, the ninth in the unbroken Chakkri Dynasty that began in 1972. As a proponent of Buddhism, and in the face of a growing and increasingly Western-style economy, he has consistently reminded his people to live with moderation and be responsible consumers. His projects to modernize and develop his country in areas such as agriculture and water conservation, as well as attempting to end poverty (most notably in Isan), have done much to bring Thailand out of the third world. It's clear why his people love him. After watching some interviews of His Majesty, I too felt enamored by his charm and intelligence.

The displays and festivals celebrating His Majesty were not limited to public spaces. The temples also took part with festooned roof lines. Gateways were strung with flashing lights and giant images of the king were lit by enormous spotlights. Wat Pramuenrat spared no expense building an altar-like structure that supported a twelve-foot-high standing image of the king who was uniformed with scabbard and dagger. In the evenings, this larger-than-life image was dazzlingly illuminated with colorful lights that reflected into my cell, reminding me of Christmas. At the time, I had no idea that a few weeks later those same lights would be reflecting off my very white and clean shaven head.

19

I had contemplated the idea of becoming a monk for some time; it almost became an obsession. It was entirely plausible as my son became older and I became increasingly dissatisfied with my American life. In those days when my departure was in its infancy in terms of planning and execution, all I could mostly think about was living, even for a short time, in pious solitude and relishing in the simplicity. I had somehow arrived at this point, and while I welcomed, and even found the idea mildly intoxicating, there were times I questioned my own sanity.

When I left my country and family across the Pacific, I tried to do it with grace and honesty. It was important to me that they understood what I was doing. This was a personal journey; a lone journey that had very little to do with the family relationship. I don't know if anyone ever really understood. I think my son, who grew up going to temple, understood more than anyone. Still, the tears that were shed on his behalf are a burden I still carry.

But I did not choose to dispose of my livelihood and cut myself off from family and friends without careful consideration or meticulous introspection. In fact, my decision was well grounded, and I had little self-doubt. I know now that many underlining factors that I hadn't been fully aware of had much to do with my state of mind.

The loss of my parents, my mother five years previously, and more recently my father, was definitely in the equation. Those were difficult times, and being far away in this temple gave me a real opportunity to mourn. A more immediate pivotal point, and one I also had no control over, was the fact that the period of my life as a parent was at its physical conclusion.

I saw leaving the United Sates as an act of survival, and in many ways, a rebirth of my own creativity. Being only in my late thirties, I saw it as an opportunity to experience and discover new things for the road ahead.

For the most part, the rest of my family, while seemingly accepting my lifestyle, were respectfully disinterested. Even so, I would have liked them to be there to share in the experience and to see this part of me.

My becoming ordained was a forgone conclusion for many of the people I had come to know. Phra Samboen frequently asked as his face positively beamed, "Ajarn Bill, all monks want to know. When you become monk? I want to eat with you."

Usually when I was asked, and I was asked a lot, I would simply indicate that I didn't know yet, but that it was a possibility.

I'll never forget the day Abbot Sunthorn invited me to become ordained. After lunch, Phra Suwatt, Luang Por, and I were relaxing in the shade when Phra Suwatt informed me that in the coming weeks the temple would be hosting an annual "King's ordination." This is a special period during which males who are unable to stay in robes because of responsibilities, such as civil servants or teachers, can enter a special program of temporary ordination. Very few temples are allowed the distinction of ordaining in the name of His Majesty. Fewer still, especially in Isan, are in the habit of ordaining foreigners.

During the meal, I noticed a different, more serious tone to their conversation. My Thai had improved, at least to the point when I could usually tell when they were talking about me. Key words such as "Ajarn" and "falang" were usually good indicators. Still, I was taken aback when Phra Suwatt turned to me and asked, "Luang Por want to know if you want to be a monk. Luang Por says you are very lucky because only he can make you Isan monk. He say he loves Ajarn Bill and you will be a beautiful monk. How do you feel?"

Before I could answer, I turned to Luang Por. He was not smiling. This was not a joke.

I had been formally invited to take part in an ancient tradition I knew little about, in a culture not my own. I was, of course, elated and incredibly excited at the very prospect. Under the circumstances, I thought it would be best if I spent some time thinking about it. With a deep wai of appreciation, I turned to Luang Por and said, "Luang Por, it would be an honor to be ordained in your temple, but this decision should not be made without careful thought. Because of this, I need to spend some time thinking about it."

As I sat listening while Phra Suwatt submitted my response, it occurred to me that I may have, in the Asian sense of politeness, somehow offended Luang Por after his very gracious offer. This turned out to be completely wrong because the moment Phra Suwatt finished translating, Luang Por slapped me on the knee and launched into such a rapid litany of Thai that it is still being translated.

In the end, they both agreed that I should be, without a doubt, ordained as the first White monk of Wat Pramuenrat.

"Oh ... Ajarn Bill you make Luang Por and all monks so happy."

Feeling an immediate need for solitude, I thanked them both and promptly excused myself. Walking back to my cell, I was in such a state that I had forgotten to gather the leftovers for the dogs. Over the months, they developed a Pavlovian response when I returned from lunch, and greeted me with yelps of anticipation while waiting from the fringes of their territory. Instead of returning to the lunch mat, I threw them some bean-filled Chinese cakes from my battered fridge which, after viciously fighting over, they left rotting in the sun.

It seemed that a moment had arrived for me, and yet it was not the romantic discovery I had always imagined. Maybe it was the way Luang Por slapped me on the knee, or how easily the whole notion of becoming a monk had simply fallen together. At the same time, though, the fact that it was so uncomplicated made me wonder if fate might be playing a part.

That evening, I went into Cho Ho and bought flowers for Luang Por's altar. I would place these into two bronze vases flanking his Buddha image. Marking the event in this way, I hoped to convey my deep gratitude and respect for him. I chose a typical offering arrangement of purple and white orchids from a street vendor across from the language school. As I walked past her school, I wondered about Ajarn Pooh and what she would think of my plans. I imagined it would only confirm her belief that the American had been foolishly hoodwinked by a bunch of monks, monks who "do not understand real life." You can imagine my surprise when a few days later she offered to personally sponsor my ordination.

Ordination is a very auspicious moment for Thai families and is taken very seriously. They revel in the opportunity to sponsor their loved ones and believe by doing so they and their ancestors will earn merit.

The family or sponsor of a newly ordained monk is responsible for most of the initial things he will need. The main item of monks robes, are offered during an elaborate ceremony. Other sundries include toiletries, candles, and packets of black tea. These are typically sold in cellophane-covered orange buckets from a wide variety of tiny shops, as well as grocery and department stores.

20

Phra Maha, the curio monk, emerges long after the bell from his cell and rubbing the sleep from his eyes, stretches his well-fed body. A temple boy sweeps the grounds around the front of his cell. Later his 'friend' or another stunner of a Thai girl will do the dishes he's left souring in an enamel wash bowl. A foreign man, who has decided to live here for the moment, will drive him anywhere he desires.

Sometimes the foreign man feels like the butt of an elaborate joke, seeking, like many before him, solace in the East. But the foreign man, who is admittedly naive and romantic almost to a fault, sees more than he should. Still, the foreign man, like a stubborn prospector, refuses to leave the hole that he's already dug for himself. In the glory of his pursuit, albeit somewhat blinded by the single point in his mind that holds out hope for a discovery, he joins them. Wrapped up tight in orange cloth and with a new determination, he continues digging.

Since being at the temple I had gotten quite good at keeping things from myself, certain revelations and cultural oddities, not the least of which was the simple fact that monks and Thai Buddhism were rather disappointing in many ways. The big question now was, "Did I allow these 'disappointments' to undermine my own practice or beliefs?" Perhaps I wanted proof or evidence that Buddhism was somehow better than Christianity and that it was more fulfilling and purer in its simplicity.

I now looked at Thailand through different eyes from when I first arrived. It was not the charming paradise that once enamored me. The smiles no longer disarmed me. The Buddhist monks I used to look upon with such deep admiration, with the exception of a few, no longer stirred my spirit with inspiration.

I hated myself for arriving at this point and even more so for allowing myself to feel so self-righteous. What did I really know about this country anyway? I was just another ignorant foreigner on the "yellow brick road," and somewhere, tucked deep into the forest, was a small man behind a curtain.

I wished Phra Maha Nikhom were there; maybe he could explain it to me. Maybe there was something I was missing, or maybe I was just full of shit. I wondered what he would think of that. I also wondered how honest I could be about my experiences. I'm sure nothing I had seen was news to him, and yet he allowed me to come. I know what I imagined for myself, but I would ask him what he imagined for me and what lessons he had hoped I would learn.

Maybe these very questions were at the root of it, that sending me to his country was his way of teaching yet another disgruntled and spiritually bankrupt American that there is no spiritual utopia or geographical cure for any of us. "Boy," he says, "life is suffering all the time. You know?"

The next morning, one of the biggest natural disasters in recorded history eradicated some two hundred thousand lives across Southeast Asia. Hundreds of miles from the South, I awoke and almost immediately sensed that something was different. There was a palpable lack of energy in the air as if I had been suddenly thrust into a different atmosphere. The village, which was normally at full tilt with the sounds of roosters, dogs, and children, lay eerily silent.

At university that afternoon, I had an exhausting lesson trying to explain to the monks why tsunami, despite the *t*, is pronounced sunami, and despite their usual compliancy, they refused to accept "because" for an answer. "Ajarn Bill, America have Tee-sunami?" It was certainly big news. To my dismay, however, most of the discussion surrounding the tsunami centered on the amazing accounts of how big the wave was and not on the fact that thousands of people had perished.

21

I found it ironic that even while living in a Buddhist temple, I still got a little stressed out. I had much to do the week before the school break and His Majesty's Birthday, the least of which was a thick stack of midterms that needed to be graded by week's end. Luang Por had scheduled a meeting with Phra Suwatt one evening. While sitting at my desk, I heard Phra Maha summon me from his window. Refusing to submit, and completely out of character, I took a deep breath, slipped on my headphones, and blocked Phra Maha with the much more favorable sounds of Miles Davis. Praise be to Miles!

Later on my way to see Luang Por, Phra Maha, with a definite air of one slighted, confronted me as I passed his open cell. "Ajarn Bill, earlier I called for you and you did not come see me. Where did you go?"

"Oh, I'm sorry, I had my headphones on. I must not have heard you. Did you knock?

"Hmm ... well, I need a ride to MCU this evening to meet with my professor, but it's OK. We can go now."

"I'm sorry, Phra Maha, I can't go, I have to meet with Luang Por and Phra Suwatt."

"Oh, no problem Ajarn, he will wait for you. We won't be long."

"Ah ... Is there any way we can go tomorrow? I really have a lot to do here tonight. I have to finish grade..."

"It's OK, Ajarn," he said turning to enter his cell, "For your happiness."

I stood dumbstruck as he returned to his cell and emphatically locked his door with a resounding thunk. I was off the hook, but with a lingering taste of wet metal.

It seemed the more I got to know Phra Maha, or perhaps the more comfortable he became taking advantage of me, the less I liked him. The close proximity of our relationship, and the fact that I had allowed him to run me, was very concerning to me. It concerned me because any relationship that starts out with one person having a clearly defined power over another makes is difficult to change or, in my case, neutralize the dynamic. Phra Maha was taught to believe that he was extraordinary; he truly saw himself as the "great monk." Phra Maha, regardless of his robes, is one of the most arrogant humans I've ever met. Likewise, Thai monks in general hold themselves above ordinary people. Much of this has to do with the way "ordinary" Thais shower them with almost royal treatment. The first time I drove Luang Por through the village, I was astonished when people along the roadside, upon seeing the temple van approach, dropped to the ground with hands clasped reverently. I could see how some could fall victim to this level of admiration and power. Abbott

Sunthorn, not to his credit but as expected, is a humble and "good monk."

Of the few open conversations I've had with Thai people, it seems that they are quite aware that there are "good monks" and "bad monks." After Ajarn Pooh learned I was living in a temple, she made reference to the "bad monks," and even advised me to be cautious about with whom I place my trust.

"Ajarn", she said, "not *all* monks are good; some go to temple because they have problems with drugs, and sometimes even criminals use the temples to hide. I know you maybe think because they are monks they are good, but it's not always true. I tell you this because I worry about these things. I think Wat Pramuenrat is a good temple, but Luang Por is getting old and cannot see everything that goes on." I used to think Ajarn Pooh had some sort of axe to grind, but when I really think about it, I realize she may have been right.

Seated across from Luang Por during our meeting, I peered deeply into his eyes. I wondered what it would be like to see through them. I also looked for evidence upon his nimble and somehow youthful hands as they gracefully moved about the folds of his robes. His hands had not caressed or held a woman in their embrace in the forty years since he was ordained, or perhaps ever. At some point, this good monk had crossed the threshold of human sensuality to a place of peace and inner harmony.

Phra Suwatt, another "good monk," joined us. After seating himself on the floor, he said to me, "Ajarn Bill, Luang Por want to see you to talk about being a monk." Luang Por enthusiastically began to animate again the act of shaving my head and eyebrows.

As Luang Por leaned in, he spoke in earnest tones while gently placing his hands in a fatherly manner upon my knee. He spoke only a few words and concluded with "I love you."

"Ajarn," said Phra Suwatt, "Luang Por say you are son to him, and he is very happy to see you tonight. Next week, you should stop working and stay in temple. After two days will have ceremony for new monk. Luang Por say I will help you understand."

"Thank you, Phra Suwatt, that's good to know because I have no idea what to do. Also, I was wondering how many new monks will be here?"

Thinking for a moment Phra Suwatt said, "have many policemen that stay for three weeks then go back to job and family."

"Can they stay longer if they want to; is that OK?" I asked.

"Hmm ... Can, yes; sometimes man stay forever, but most go back to family."

"What will happen, or what will we do exactly after the ceremony?"

Phra Suwatt referred the question to Luang Por and then answered, "Too many things Ajarn. Get up early to beg for food, chanting and meditation all day. Don't worry Ajarn, you will be beautiful monk and bring merit to your parents."

22

The month of December brought the monotonous heat and stillness to an abrupt halt. The glutinous heat lingering upon the Khorat plateau was washed away and replaced with a cool and unexpected crispness.

The transformation to the cool season invigorated me and reminded me of the Midwestern autumn of my youth: the aroma of wool while pulling on a sweater, the oaken wet smell of piled leaves, and the comforting warmth of my mother's hands removing wet socks, embracing cold feet. These thoughts invigorated me. With an unseen support that I knew my mother was sending, I had a renewed sense of rightness.

Accommodating my reflective spirit, all of the monks, with the exception of Phra Maha, Phra Suwatt, and Luang Por, left for a ten-day retreat at the university. I was sincerely glad. It felt good to have the temple to myself. I needed this time to mentally prepare for what was coming.

Arming myself with a bamboo broom, I wandered through the deserted temple to sit quietly by the lake. On the way, I stopped briefly to glance at the bell tower girl. At the bath house I listen for the usual splash of water and slamming doors. The doors were ajar and the only sounds were a rank of dripping taps drumming rust spots into the calcified cisterns. Rounding the corner of the bath house, I tapped my stick against the cracked concrete and announced my arrival to the bitch and her now equally aggressive den of much larger pups. She feigned an advance, but as usual, quickly retreated. I would see her again on my way back, where we would repeat our show of individual dominance.

As I walked the thin dirt path along the lake, a cool breeze swayed the tops of the tamarind trees, sending slender brown pods earthbound. A moment later, the bamboo grove responded in a chorus of painful creaks and groans as the towering green pendulums gently crashed into and chafed one another.

Before modern plumbing, temples were a main source of water for many of the villages, so for that purpose nearly every temple has a body of water. The lake at Wat Pramuenrat, which is really a large pond, was not the place of reflection or beauty you might imagine a temple lake to be. The docks were crumbled and partially sunken, and the water was dotted with an assortment of floating and half-submerged plastic bags. In the dry season, the receded water level revealed tangles of busted furniture and hundreds of mud-glazed bottles.

As I walked along the thin path, I spied a turtle perched upon a jutting branch from the water's surface. Stopping along the trash-strewn bank to look, I began thinking, and it occurred to me that as far as the turtle was concerned, this lake was perfectly acceptable. At that moment, squatting at the water's edge full of my opinions, "I" was out of the equation. What *I thought* was of no consequence; my opinion pointless and empty.

Afterward, whenever I walked along the lake side, I tried to focus my mind not on those imperfect things but instead on the beauty of my surroundings: the creaking bamboo, the tamarind trees, and the turtles sunning themselves. Maybe the practice of Buddhism is to live with grace in a world filled with crumbling docks and discarded plastic. Are we not turtles, perched precariously on a branch, in an imperfect world?

23

On the west coast, the sun rises above the rose-dyed peaks of the Cascades. On street corners, coffee roasters send out the mornings first aromatic tendrils of justifiably overpriced coffee. In the city, a metro sexual parks his Saab for twenty dollars a day. Along the waterfront, a homeless man holds up a large sign that asks, "Are You Going to Hell?"

In Thailand, there's a bowl upon my lap that is quickly filling with my hair. The cleanly shaved ridges above my eyes are cool and smooth. A chilling drop of water is rolling down the small of my back. Next to me are another bowl and another man. I want to turn my head and look, but I don't want Phra Suwatt to accidentally cut me. Around me are a few dozen people; many are from the village. With scissors in hand, they deftly share in the cutting, placing a sheared ribbon of my former vanity into my bowl. We are bare to the waist. Hairy sheets of suds fold away and fall dripping down our bare shoulders as the razors plow our scalps. Because I have chest hair, something of a novelty to Thai people who have no qualms in pointing this out, I feel an uneasy modesty. Sensing this, Luang Por drapes a cool white sheet around me.

The twenty-five police officers who arrived the day before did not speak to me, and despite my initial efforts, their collective lack of congeniality was palpable. When I approached, their eyes perused me as though searching for certain evidence of my flawed character. I took comfort in the fact that I had a private cell in which to escape their blank faces. I wanted to tell them that even with their heads shaved, they still looked like a bunch of cops.

ith heads and brows shaved and dressed in white novice robes, the twenty-five novice cops congregated with their families. Their robes were elegant and beautifully made of delicate silk needlepoint. Standing on the fringes with my simple white sheet, I watched as mothers with proud tears in their eyes fussed around them while posing for photos taken mostly with cell phone cameras.

There was a time I would have enjoyed the spectacle of a Thai ceremony (and it is a spectacle), however, after witnessing so many, I now find the pomp tiresome and tend to avoid them altogether. With my sheet snugly around my wet neck, I made my way through the throng of onlookers and novices who gawked and whispered as I passed. I wanted nothing more than for this day to end.

Before I could escape to my cell, I saw Luang Por uncharacteristically walk briskly from his cell. Coming towards me, he gestured excitedly for me to follow. Through the throng once again, which parted into an avenue before us, he led me to his cell. Once inside, he closed the door, removed my sheet, and vanished into his back chamber.

Bare to the waist, and glad for the refuge of the darkened cell, I gazed through the glass doors as the people joyfully trouped past. The white-robed and bald police officers milled about; their formerly smug expressions now somewhat dazed.

When Luang Por returned to me in the outer chamber, he carried in his hands bolts of folded silk: one a rich deep green and another pale gold. Raising my arms, he wrapped the green silk around my waist, which was heavy and cool against my skin. Like a tailor, he frequently paused to survey the cut before grunting in satisfaction. He then unfolded and lowered a pale golden sash upon my shoulder. Lastly, he removed my watch before opening his cell doors and leading me out into the sun.

Phra Suwatt, who evidently had been waiting on the porch, looked upon me as I exited. Shaking his head, he said, "Oh... Ajarn, so beautiful. Luang Por gives you very special Indian silk. You very lucky." I felt regal as Phra Suwatt led me by the arm to present me, a now-complete novice, to the people.

For the next hour, we mingled and posed for pictures while greeting one another shyly but with great kindness and Thai gentleness. Mothers and old women, standing at arm's length so as not to touch, clapped their hands and gasped with joy.

In conclusion of the novice ceremony, the people led us to circle the bot three times in homage to the Buddha, the *dhamma*, and the *sangha*, or the Buddha, the "truth," and the "community of monks." In their fervor, the people informed the spirit world of our ordination with great howls at each passing while a trio of old men, their heads colorfully bound in Isan silk, performed traditional Thai music, sawing and screeching out a medley of joyous celebration. Feeling I was indeed part of this, I reminded myself to savor the smiles, the feeling of the Indian silk against my skin, and the cool beading sweat on my brow.

24

The next morning, tangled in my lower robe, I awoke before the bell. Leaving the lights off, I lit the candles in front of my Buddha for the illusion of warmth. Today would be a very long and a very Thai day. Most of what I would experience I probably wouldn't understand, but my main concern, apart from not looking foolish, was not doing something inadvertently disrespectful.

Putting on my sash, I went out to the garden to greet the day and mentally prepare myself. Wandering there in my decadence amongst the flowers, I must have been quite the sight. An old woman, making her way along the outer wall, stopped to peer in at me through the decorative spaces in the brick. Smiling, she muttered excitedly, gave me a respectful wai, and shuffled off while giggling down the lane.

Turning from this encounter, I caught a glimpse of Phra Suwatt entering my porch. I called out to him, "Good morning, Phra Suwatt, I'm out here."

"Oh, Ajarn what are you doing?"

"Just sitting here," I answered.

"You okay?" he asked, smiling.

"Yes, I'm fine," I replied.

"Luang Por want me to make sure."

"I'm good Phra Suwatt, thank you; a little nervous but OK."

"Ajarn, today will be long day, but I will help you so do not worry about speaking Thai."

"Thank you. I am a little worried about that."

"I think so," said Phra Suwatt, slowly nodding his head.

"Go to sala when bell, maybe one hour. Okay?"

"Okay, I'll see you there."

Thanking him with a very heartfelt and appreciative wai, I watched as he briskly departed down the path.

I sincerely liked Phra Suwatt, but sadly our relationship, which had always been cordial, did not have the sensations of true friendship. Sometimes when I looked at him, I could see plainly that he was mentally somewhere else; maybe at home with his family, or perhaps far away from this temple and his unrelenting responsibilities as secretary. I was also acutely aware that he had a certain, and often palpable, disdain for Phra Maha. I wouldn't exactly say Phra Suwatt was jealous of Phra Maha, but, in my opinion, his disdain seemed to lie mostly in the fact that Phra Maha got away with doing very little actual work in the temple.

My close proximity to Phra Maha, and the fact that I was once so obviously taken by his charm, probably has much to do with Phra Suwatt remaining distant from me. There is much I would like to say to him regarding my relationship with Phra Maha, but unfortunately it's not my place and my doing so would only cause unnecessary conflict. Nevertheless, I have the feeling and the belief that Phra Maha's karma will arrive without my intervention.

Twenty minutes later, I was summoned by the bell. I braced myself with three deep breaths and walked over to the sala. I had been aware of the commotion in the front of the temple but was in no way prepared for the mass of people who had gathered there. Dumbfounded by the intense surroundings, I followed the other novices inside. On the floor of the sala were ranks of sitting mats, and located next to each of these was a single monk's bowl. We filed in, and closed ranks among the mats, and took our places next to a single bowl. With our legs tucked under, we sat quietly on the floor as the people milled about taking pictures.

With legs tucked and hands in prayer, we twenty-six novices sat as Luang Por presided over the opening ceremony with an opening chant. This chant was one of the few I knew well enough to take part in as it was commonly done before and after meditation.

After chanting, a host of monks, including Phra Maha and guest monks from other temples, took turns speaking. Some of these were abbots who were there as witnesses. This went on for a torturous hour or so and I have no idea what was said. Just as the searing pain of my near gangrenous legs traveled into my lower back, everyone turned to face their bowl. Alongside the bowls sat the families, or in my case, my sponsor. Facing this throng of onlookers, I soon realized that Ajarn Pooh was not present, but instead sent her aunt as a proxy, who observed and grinned with affection. I smiled as she placed a folded set of robes atop my bowl, topping them with a single purple orchid.

Carrying our robes, we then proceeded reverently in single file to meet Luang Por under the outdoor pavilion in what is called 'going forth.' I was thankful that Phra Suwatt, who had neglected to instruct me on this very important moment, hurried up to my side and whispered, "Ajarn, do what other monk do, okay?"

Nodding my head, I asked with restrained panic, "What do I say to Luang Por? Some of the other monks seem to be saying something."

"Don't say anything here. No problem."

Waiting my turn, I watched carefully as each new monk walked forth and gently handed Luang Por their robes, which he blessed and immediately handed back. After pausing at Luang Por's request for a photo, I did the same. With blessed robes in hand, and Phra Suwatt at my side breathing a heavy sigh of relief, we made our way back into the sala.

Inside, behind an improvised curtain of monk's robes, we removed our novice gowns and redressed in our saffron robes. The robes are not one piece, but consist of many pieces sewn together like a patchwork. This pattern is strictly followed, regardless of the color or material. Legend has it that the sewn pattern represents the rice paddies of Magadha in Northern India. They have the feel of freshly laundered bed sheets. I was happy to discover there was no confining undergarment, only a lower robe which is secured by a rope and web belt, also the color of saffron. I felt remarkably comfortable and much cooler than I expected.

We stood like patient children as the monks hovered around us, tucking and adjusting hems and folds. Smiling, I was able to make brief eye contact with some of the former police officers and could see for a moment that perhaps they were humbled, and even charged, by the moment. Others, though, seemed glum and disaffected.

There was one officer who, unlike the others, was comfortable holding my gaze. He looked upon me much in the same way as Poo Yai did when I first met him, with great suspicion. Later in the week, I discovered him as he attempted to covertly photograph me with his cell phone camera.

The final step completing our ordination took place in the bot. This was a much smaller building than the sala but similar in function. In this place, each of us would meet privately with Luang Por, two other local abbots, and eleven other monks who acted as witnesses for what is essentially a final examination and confirmation of suitability.

Entering the bot, I was greeted warmly by the seated monks who smiled and nodded approvingly as I made my way to kneel in front of Luang Por. Tilting his head back slightly, as though surveying his work, he did not smile but pursed his lips in a thoughtful, but no less approving fashion. I was then asked the three questions all monks have been asked throughout the ages:

Are you suffering from any disease such as leprosy, boils, ringworm, tuberculosis, or any other diseases?

Are you a human being?

Are you a free man, free from debt, and twenty years or older, and do you have your family's permission?

Answering these questions I then repeated after Luang Por the request for acceptance. This is called *Upasamapada*, and it was followed by the chanted confirmation and announcement of my ordination, which was done three times. Finally, I was given the new Pali name of *Phra Sukkumalo*, which means "grace and order" when translated in English.

As we left the bot now fully ordained, the villagers greeted each of us with howls of praise. The air was showered with fistfuls of candy and coins, which the children snatched from the ground around our feet. Phra Sukkumalo was now a monk.

With our ordination complete, the music abruptly stopped. Motorcycles roared to life and the temple was quickly deserted. We twenty-six newly ordained monks retreated to our cells without further ceremony. In my cell, I lazed upon the floor, limpid and exhausted, and repeated my name, "*Phra Sukkumalo, Phra Sukkumalo, Phra Sukkumalo.*" Was I really a monk?

In the morning, I awoke at four. I had about twenty minutes before the bell to bathe and properly dress myself. Oddly enough, that was about the same time I had while in basic training for the U.S. Navy. It was too cold for a bucket bath so I began to struggle with my robes. I had tried the night before to remove them as carefully as possible in the hope of easing myself into them. This was done in vain because I had no idea which end was up.

Robes require skill and concentration when folding. It took me almost until the end of my time as an actual monk before I could do so without assistance. The outer robe, or *sanghati*, is the most difficult. It's a bit larger than a king-size bed sheet when unfolded. The sanghati must be folded lengthwise into a long rectangle, laid over the left shoulder, and then unfolded enough to wrap around body and be tucked under the left arm. The inner garment, or *ungsa*, is two parts consisting of a thin undershirt that is cut to expose the right arm, and a bottom robe, or *sabong*, which is basically double-folded around the waist, very much like a skirt, and secured with a web belt. It is the easiest part to put on.

We wore full or "formal" robes the majority of the time, however, they but could be worn in different ways depending on the circumstances. During work periods we were allowed to wear just the undershirt and lower robe, which are very comfortable and well ventilated. Everything regarding clothing and hygiene involved the colors yellow, brown, saffron, and orange. This included bath towels, washcloths, wash buckets, and bedding. It also included umbrellas, and in cold weather, stocking caps or socks.

The only article that is not persistently "yellow" is the monk's bag. These bags, which are used to carry personal items and food during alms rounds, are extraordinarily beautiful. Most identify a temple with an insignia or logo elaborately embroidered on them. The bags are commonly made from choice silk and handcrafted. Ours were crafted in a rich green silk, but I've seen nearly every color, even hot pink.

With a scant few minutes before the summoning bell, and no hope of dressing myself properly, I bunched up my robes. Bare-chested and positively stressed, I went out into the dark and cold temple in search of aid. In doing so, I terrified my dog who leapt from the porch with a terrified yelp, no doubt shocked by the unexpected sight of me.

Phra Maha was my first thought, but he wouldn't be up for another five or six hours. Then I saw the flickering of candles in the dorm next door. Those monks were a group who seldom spoke to me, even if I addressed them. They weren't unfriendly, just very shy. Without much choice, I gently knocked upon the outer door and waited as a heavy lock was freed from its clasp. Creaking open the door, a young monk stood wide-eyed as I apologetically held up my robes with a look of great defeat.

Understanding my plea for assistance, he smiled and beckoned me in. Entering, I noticed that unlike mine, his cell was no larger than that of an average prison. On the floor was a partially folded sleeping mat, a low table, and below the unscreened window, a Buddha image surrounded by kidney-shaped puddles of yellow wax. Standing in the warm glow of his tiny cell, we spoke not a word; the only sounds were the soft flutter of cotton and gentle padding as he folded, wrapped, and quickly tucked me into a snug monastic cocoon. Thanking him profusely, I left him smiling and nodding in the warmth of his little cell just as the bell struck.

Still dark and with bowl in hand, I made my way barefoot across the grounds to the sala. With a cool breeze tickling my tender foreign feet, I stood for a moment to gaze upwards through the canopy at the morning stars. Standing there in that moment, I had the feeling that I had, at the very least, accomplished something.

Arriving at the still-darkened sala, I realized that my haste was completely unnecessary. I even startled Phra Suwatt, who, with a jangling set of keys, had come to open the building.

"Ajarn?" he said, taking a step back in the darkness. "You here now?"

"Good morning, Phra Suwatt. I thought we had to be here when the bell rang."

"Yes, but many monks here so maybe not start on time." Smiling, he continued, "How did you put your robe on so good?"

"I had to get help. I had no idea," I said.

Laughing, he said, "I think many new monks also."

With the sala opened, I walked among the two long rows of yellow carpeted sitting mats. Settling down upon mat number six, I tucked my robes under my legs against the cold and meditated until the others arrived. Concentrating on the night sounds, I again reminded myself to keep an open mind and to use this opportunity to its fullest.

Filing in and sitting around me, the police monks giggled and chatted among themselves. I nodded, but I was met with mostly blank stares and weak grunts.

The morning session in the sala lasted for about an hour. We spent the majority of this time chanting and about twenty minutes in meditation. The chanting was hard for me and I didn't enjoy it. Phra Suwatt gave me a translated version of the chants, but since they didn't match what the others were saying, I had no idea what I was saying, therefore defeating the very purpose of his assistance. Still, I knew a few chants and mouthed those along with the others as best I could.

It was still dark when we emerged from the sala. Outside, Phra Suwatt organized us into groups for our first alms rounds, or *pindabat.* With bowls in hand and in single file, we walked solemnly from the gate and into the fetid streets. As we walked along, the people stood quietly in front of their homes and shop houses. When we stopped, they placed heaping ladles of hot rice into each of our bowls. Many also offered curries and other dishes which were sealed inside the ubiquitous clear plastic bag which serves as the 'to go' method in Thailand. Sealed tightly with a rubber band, these often swell up like small food balloons, occasionally exploding their unidentified contents. It's perhaps the most unappetizing presentation of food you could imagine.

As I moved through the cold morning, the rising sun warmed my exposed right shoulder. The warmth of the rice in my bowl against my belly was pleasing. Barefoot, I stepped in all manner of organic substances. The gouged and cratered pavement was cold and scoured my soft Western feet, which were quickly bruised and bloody. I found this oddly stimulating, perhaps because it was so undeniably real.

Nothing was said as we moved through the awakening villages. Our lead monk, who is Phra Suwatt's cell mate, frequently gave us advice on how to properly receive offerings.

Without speaking, he showed me how to properly tip my bowl so as to avoid touching the women's hands. When the last bowl in line was filled, we offered no thanks and made no eye contact. A chanted blessing was given, and without another word or gesture, we departed.

As we moved through the streets, our bowls, which did not hold more than one liter or so, were quickly filled. We also carried a silken orange temple bag to carry other food stuffs like chicken, assorted curries, and wrapped items. Temple boys and volunteers patrolled in our wake to relieve us by tipping our warm parcels of rice, which had settled into round steaming plugs, into large wicker baskets.

Returning from alms rounds, we found the temple alive with activity. People from the village came to help with the meal; there was a feeling of community spirit. Returning, we dumped the last of our rice and rinsed our bowls for breakfast. Some mornings, I had time for a short rest and a quick foot bath. Other mornings, my group returned last, and I had just enough time to rinse my alms bowl and take my seat.

My first morning, we were out collecting alms for more than two hours. My feet were in bad shape by the time we entered the gate. I noticed as we walked through the gate that the other monks had left their sandals there in neat little rows. I left mine in front of my cell, forcing me to walk the remaining three hundred yards of unpaved gravel. I wouldn't do that again.

Gathering together to rinse their bowls, a few of the police monks gave me a thumbs-up. Nodding, I smiled and returned the gesture. I guess I passed some sort of test in their eyes. I made a note to remind myself that I had nothing to prove to them and that I was not there for their entertainment. I had been living there for ten months like a monk. Maybe I had a bad attitude, but something about those men prompted me to mind my own business.

Because of His Majesty's birthday, offerings to temples tended to increase in volume and in quality. Breakfast, which I typically avoided before I became ordained, was an absolute feast of Thai delicacies. There were now omelets, Chinese cakes, and even fried chicken.

On the rare mornings that we returned from rounds with time to spare, I hustled back to my cell to tend to my feet and have a few moments of reflection. In my bathroom, I poured bucket after bucket of water over my feet. Since it was the cool season, the water was very cold. I hadn't taken a bucket bath in days. Outside, I rounded the corner to my garden. I got a nice bit of morning sun there. I felt remarkably odd as I sat against the outside wall of my cell. Slanting over the temple wall was a wide beam of sunshine. Warming my feet in the rays, I listened to the sounds of the village: children laughing, dogs barking, and motorcycles roaring. I suddenly realized how weird my life had become.

Sitting down to breakfast, I felt refreshed and ready for the long morning ahead. During meals, the new monks were delegated to a separate section of tables at the end of the eating area, while the other monks, the full-time monks I feel comfortable with, sat nearer the front. Whenever I sat with the police monks, there was a palpable tension I cannot describe, and although I knew they couldn't possibly have a reason to hate me, they seemed to be very uncomfortable in my presence. Because of this, I attempted to sit as close to them as possible. Some mornings, I found myself squeezed between two portly monks, and other mornings, whoever I was seated near went out of their way to make extra room for me. Phra Maha said this wasn't a sign of hatred of any kind, but simply to avoid the embarrassment of conversing with me in English. It was to my benefit, though, as I tended to have an entire grouping of food bowls to myself.

In the temple, and in typical Thai fashion, food bowls are shared by all those present. If I wanted something, I stuck my spoon in, took a few pieces, and then placed it into my bowl. Soup was shared in the same way. At first, all this spoon dipping seemed unsanitary, but in time, I quit thinking about it. None of the food we collected was reheated, but it was so spicy hot it hardly mattered.

On a typical morning, I might have in front of me soup, whole fish, pork dishes, sticky rice, and a variety of sauces containing some combination of hot peppers and fish sauce. The dessert bowls overflowed with coconut milk, mangos, and sticky rice, as well as a variety of bakery goods.

A monk's food, in the true sense of tradition, is neither judged by its presentation or flavor. Its purpose is to merely sustain the body. In forest temples, you eat once each day of whatever is placed in your alms bowl and that's all you get. Sometimes, I had to remind myself not to make any judgments regarding what I like or don't like. There were some things, such as the common fermented fish sauce, for which I simply couldn't acquire a taste.

After breakfast, we all walked over to the sala for three hours of lecture, meditation, and of course, more chanting. These were long days for me. Sitting through the lectures, which were in Thai, seemed to last an eternity, and since I understood practically none of it, they were especially grueling. Phra Maha's lectures were particularly torturous as he seemed to enjoy the sound of his own voice. I loved nothing more than when he stopped talking and we began meditation.

Aside from a brief evening break when we were served fruit juice by the temple boys, there was no leisure time in our schedule. Every hour, with the exception of lunch and the afternoon work period, was spent seated upon the sala floor.

Because I was continually frustrated with the fact that I wasn't benefiting from the dharma lectures, I consulted Phra Suwatt. He suggested I receive these same lectures in English from Phra Maha. I was relieved to be getting out of the sala. I was also hopeful that Phra Maha would take the opportunity to redefine our relationship and perhaps show me how great he *really* was. Unfortunately, my dharma lesson consisted of us sitting around his cell while he either chatted on the phone or pecked away at his keyboard.

Instruction each day ended at nine o'clock in the evening. Leaving the sala, the police monks headed off to their dormitory while I went alone to my cell in another direction. In the bathroom, I found the cold water in the bath bucket heavenly. I dumped several buckets over my head, leaving the gushing tap to pummel my feet. Too cold in the morning to bathe, it felt good to wash the dust from my eyes and the filth from my aching feet.

Wearing only the lower garment like a saffron kilt, I was cool and very comfortable as I lounged upon my sleeping mat. In a state of limpid meditation, I reflected on my day and the harsh realities of monk-hood. My feet hurt badly, and because we only ate two meals, the last of which was nearly ten hours earlier, I was hungry. It was not what anyone would consider fun. I was happy, though. It was a deeper happiness than a good meal or a sturdy pair of shoes could ever provide.

I had a lot of sturdy shoes and all the food I could eat in the United States. I had a nice house in a nice community and all the comforts of Western living. From my home studio, I taught a solid base of returning students. Throughout the week, I performed with various working jazz groups and occasionally enjoyed the pleasures of a traveling musician. By all accounts, that was a good life. Other than the fact that I could have used the income of stardom, it was exactly what I had always wanted. Why, then, did it become so utterly pointless and creatively draining?

Things were so much simpler here. I didn't have any bills, debt, or possessions to worry about. I knew at some point I'd have to rejoin the human race. How I ran that race would be totally up to me, but hopefully with the wisdom to keep it simple. For now, though, I tried to keep my mind on those moments. What I would do after I left the temple, whether it was returning to music or living in Thailand, I hadn't the faintest idea.

25

As a Buddhist, I believe in karma and to some extent, even reincarnation. I don't believe, as the Thai do, that my family or ancestors will receive benefits or merit because I became a monk. I'm not even sure I will.

The fixation on death and accruing merit for the next life are an integral part of Thai Buddhism. When death is confronted, it is done so delicately.

Wat Pramuenrat has on average two funerals a month with our monks in mostly full attendance. The services, or pre-cremation ceremonies, are exceedingly drawn-out affairs that can last well into the night. These services involve monks who are employed for the sole purpose of chanting. Of course, these monks aren't directly paid, but rather, a contribution is given and then the money is doled out accordingly. I once made a hundred baht just for showing up to huge funeral for a Chinese Thai that lasted three days.

I even had the honor of taking part in a up country funeral, which was an experience I'll never forget. I'm aware of how morbid it may sound, but when Phra Maha explained we were both going to head up country for a funeral at his aunt's house, I could hardly contain my excitement. Here was my first working gig as a monk and a chance to do a little travel outside the monastic confines of the wat, and for a change, I wouldn't be driving.

In the heart of Isan, the villages seem more like islands as they are surrounded by miles of checkerboard rice paddies. Arriving after sundown, I was amazed by how absolutely dark and shut down Phra Maha's village seemed. Driving slowly through the narrow lanes, we approached his family's house, which was gently illuminated by strings of Christmas lights. On a lopsided table set into the dirt yard, a flickering television mesmerized a group of small children.

As we entered the house, which was basically a concrete box with a corrugated roof, we were greeted with a flurry of wais and commotion as old women sprang into action fetching cushions and bottled water. As always, most of the children present fled behind the colorful silken skirts of their mothers when the foreigner entered.

Settling upon a thin cushion at the head of the concrete room, I sat beside Phra Maha and silently sipped my tepid water. The old Thai ladies settled down, contently chewing beetle nut and flashing smiles that were somehow still radiant through their blackened gums. Against a concrete wall that was draped with Christmas lights, a massive casket sat amid thick swirls of incense. Bedecked with yellow carnations, the casket was a decadent midnight blue, beautifully inlaid with golden Buddhas and lotus motifs that glittered and twinkled in the candlelight. Sitting in this simple concrete room, it seemed, in a word, royal.

Phra Maha said the body had been in his aunt's house for several days. "Keeping the body in the house, the family can mourn and pray, bringing merit to the deceased and peace to the family. When the monks come they pray and perform special chanting for the dead," he explained.

Phra Maha and I sat as still and quiet as stones for about forty five minutes. We didn't do any chanting or praying for anyone. Our presence here seemed simply that, a presence. All around us, small groups of family members sat quietly on the barren floor, old ladies meticulously masticated beetle nut, and outside on a poorly receiving television, a Thai game show, complete with slide whistle, pierced the night.

Afterward, we took a long walk together through the completely darkened streets of the village. While we walked, Maha fondly recalled a childhood memory of him and his father chasing field mice and frying them. The trip to Maha's village had a huge impact on me, and I felt honored, even grateful, that he asked me along.

Back in the suffering routine with my fellow monks, the days floated by with little change. During the work period, we swept the walks, rearranging the dirt, and in the sala, I still sat alone, though among them, with my thoughts.

At meals, a truly social event, the tension that used to nearly suffocate me had been replaced with my complete indifference.

My respect for them as police officers, or monks, was completely irrelevant and I began to behave as though they no longer existed.

It seems that I was continually being disappointed by many of the things I learned, and continued to learn for that matter, about Thai Buddhism. Even those men with whom I shared what I believed to be a very intimate and possibly life changing opportunity seemed to take very little of it seriously. Sitting in meditation, they freely answered cell phones, sent text messages, or simply left the sala altogether.

The next morning I woke up cold and depressed. I neglected to even try and fold my robes and perhaps in defiance, simply twisted them around my shoulders. To be honest, in the back of my mind, I knew this was a mistake. I was just growing very tired of adhering to the constant demands of form with little understanding of the function.

Warmly wrapped, I entered the sala, performed my three bows, and then sat in complete silence as I usually did. Around me, some of the police monks softly giggled, while others clicked their tongues and commented in hushed tones. Phra Suwatt, too, was less than impressed and immediately led me out to dress me as a proper monk.

"Ajarn Bill, what happened to you?" He asked clearly surprised.

Laughing, mostly because I realized how pathetic I must have looked, I simply apologized as he quickly folded me back into a proper monk.

Later, while sitting with Phra Maha, who had learned of my little stunt, I questioned him regarding the 'wearing of robes.'

"Phra Maha," I said, "the Buddha said, 'Robes are only to cover our bodies from the elements.' Why, then, do we wear them so elegantly tucked and folded, always having to adjust and fuss over them?"

"Yes, you are correct. The Buddha said that, but Thai people like beautiful monks, and this is how we must be. You must be a beautiful monk all the time," he replied.

"What if a monk is cold and wishes to wrap himself in order to be warm?"

"If a monk is cold yes, he should be warm."

"It was cold this morning when I wrapped myself."

"Yes, Ajarn, but there is a special method, and a new monk cannot wear his robes that way. You see?"

"If I am a monk and you're a monk, how is that different?"

"You are a new monk, and still learning, so you must learn how to fold the robes before you can wear them differently."

Apparently "looking" like a monk has more importance than behaving like a monk, and while I agree that a new monk should learn how to fold his robes, I don't fully understand the logic behind having to suffer in the cold for the sake of vanity. What would the Buddha think?

On the last day in robes, I found my spirits bolstered by the return of Phra Samboen and the other Khmer monks from their meditation retreat. Since none of them had seen me in robes, they came to my cell en masse, where I was greeted with warmth and badly needed friendship.

Phra Samboen, the most fluent in English among them, spoke for the group. "Teacher Bill, I am sorry, Ajarn Sukkumalo," he said, giggling. "Did you cry like baby? All monks want to know."

"No, I didn't cry."

"Really?" asked Phra Samboen, "I think so. Ajarn... Monks say you are very beautiful."

Although not a senior monk, it was to my great satisfaction that I was allowed to leave the warmth and camaraderie of the police table to spend my final days eating with my friends. Sitting with these real monks, monks that I spent nearly a year getting to know and understand, did much to improve my attitude.

"Phra Sukkumalo!" they said, calling out my name. "I am so happy we now eat food together."

Arriving at the eating area for my final meal as a monk, I was welcomed to the head tables by my returning students who rose from their seats and enthusiastically began crowding bowls of food in front of me. Beckoning me to eat, they exclaimed, "Eat a lot Ajarn!" As I sat among those monks, the monks I had laughed with and grown to know and love over the many months since my arrival, I saw the pride in their bright faces and felt at last a very real connection to a way of life and a philosophy that once seemed so out of reach. I looked briefly over to the police monks I had such a difficult time connecting with and found that for once, my gaze was held and even met with a few very genuine smiles.

26

There is a part of me, perhaps on the fringes of my heart that wanted to stay in those robes and continue living as a monk. I felt alive and more fully engaged with life than I had in such a long time, and despite certain realities that had come to pass, I was somewhat fulfilled. Months later, far from that temple and once again engaged in normal living, I would very often feel it's tug upon me. In darker moments, I sometimes wondered if I should have stayed.

At the sala for the last time, I placed my bowl upon a low table with the others. For this ceremony, there were no musicians. No one wanted to take our photo. Luang Por spoke briefly and then signifying our return to the laity, he symbolically loosened the outer belt of our robes which we then removed. Behind the improvised curtain of monk's robes we dressed ourselves back into ordinary human clothes, carelessly discarding our robes onto a central pile on the floor.

I must admit that it felt good to be wearing jeans as I left the sala. I wasn't as happy about the underwear though. The born-again cops wandered away in all directions, tucking in shirttails and rubbing their still barren scalps. Waiting cars and idle girlfriends perched upon various motorcycles welcomed them before speeding away through the open gates.

I had nowhere to go except back to the mind-bending isolation of my cell. Sitting on my mat, I mentally fumbled through the past eleven months of my life. I would like to think the time spent in this temple had somehow changed or improved my abilities to be a better human being. The truth is I really don't know. Can deep, everlasting change take place at one's command? Can a year in a temple, or anywhere for that matter, really have such an effect on a person?

But maybe this experience was just a fertile seed with a very hard casement, one that over time and under the right conditions would breach the reluctant soil of my mind and bring to bear something useful, like wisdom. Regardless, it was abundantly clear to me that my time there had reached a conclusion, not quite the elegant one I had imagined, but a conclusion nonetheless. I could stay, of course, but to do so would seem unnatural and even self-defeating.

My attitude was certainly lighter and my mind was clear. These things were wonderful, of course, but the real challenge was to maintain them, to hold on to what I felt and what I learned.

At the university, I turned in my final grades and with them, my resignation. As a foreign teacher paid a pittance, it couldn't last forever. The opportunity to teach at Mahachulalongkorn Rajvidyalaya University had been an honor. It was a privilege to be part of such an ambitious and burgeoning Buddhist university.

I will miss the hundreds of smiling monks who always greeted me with such warmth among those orange-filled corridors.

With my bags packed, I gave the garden a final watering and my dog a good, long scratch. Locking my cell door, I wandered over and took a final look at my morning nemesis, the bell tower, and the lone cracked image of the Thai girl. I wonder what she would think of all this. Maybe she was laughing at that very moment. As I turned, the leaves shuffled and gently blew across my feet. It was time to go.

At Phra Samboen's cell we had a final cup of instant coffee, and with more tension than expected, we struggled through a long and fractured goodbye. I will miss him, and I hope he knows this. He is an extraordinary monk and the very personification of compassion.

I sat with Luang Por, and without ceremony, I thanked him. Because I love him, I told him so. Pointing to the idling van, he smiled upon me and like a father, gently touched my knee. It had all been said.

Loading my bags, I looked around for Phra Maha. I wanted him to say goodbye. I, too, wanted to say goodbye. I wished I could explain to him the many things he taught me, even without his knowledge.

Phra Suwatt, always on duty, had few words. Gently clasping my forearm, he said, "Ajarn Bill, we hope you never forget Wat Pramuenrat, and all monks."

"Phra Suwatt," I said as I smiled, looking into his eyes, "there's no way I'll ever forget."

27

Long after the stubborn remnants of the temple had been scrubbed from my feet, and to my great relief, a full set of new eyebrows had grown, I found myself thinking about those days beside the garden, the soft coo of doves alighting, and Luang Por's fatherly smile. I even found myself craving, among other things, instant coffee, spicy som tom, and if I was feeling really sentimental, the odor of very old fish sauce.

Aside from the sensual, I often recalled those moments that reminded me that I had accomplished the very thing I set out to do, which was to dig deep into my own heart, into my soul, to discover new parts of what exactly I'm made of, and these things in the very purest sense were my purpose for traveling here.

Returning to Wat Pramuenrat six months later, I found in accordance with Buddhist belief that nothing is permanent. The Khmer monks, including Phra Samboen, had since left the temple and were now back home with their families in Cambodia. He and I continue to stay in touch.

Phra Suwatt still worked tirelessly as temple secretary. He has become a very dear friend and always welcomes me back to temple with the genuine warmth and camaraderie the Thai people are known for.

To his credit, Phra Maha was devoting much of his time teaching a meditation course. I attended his class at his request, and found it to be very enjoyable.

Not much had changed with my beloved Luang Por. Greeting him again much in the same way as when I first met him, I found him idly preparing his beetle nut.

The garden I had poured so much of my heart into, with the hopes of leaving at least a tiny legacy, had been re-converted to its former state. It was now once again littered with garbage, broken glass, and blackened patches of scorched soil.

To my private satisfaction, a temple boy had completely totaled the temple van during an attempted driving lesson. The front end cleaved by a steel post, it now rested, surrounded by bits of sparkling glass, in the shadow of the bell tower.

Back on the treadmill with my fellow man, I constantly remind myself that those days, those times of solitude and experience, can be anywhere in my mind if I so choose. At any moment, and there have been many, I can go back to those sweltering days upon Phra Samboen's polished floor. I can close my eyes and be back among the sons of Isan.